UNEP promotes environmentally sound practices globally and in its own activities. This publication is printed on 100 per cent recycled paper. Our distribution policy aims to reduce UNEP's carbon footprint.

SYNTHESIS REPORT
WHO/UNEP
HEALTH AND ENVIRONMENT LINKAGES INITIATIVE (HELI)

Glossary

CBA	Cost Benefit Analysis
CEA	Cost Effectiveness Analysis
DALY	Disability Adjusted Life Year
DPSEEA	Driver, Pressure, State, Exposure, Effects and Action (Framework)
EBD	Environmental Burden of Disease
EIA	Environmental Impact Assessment
HELI	Health and Environment Linkages Initiative
HIA	Health Impact Assessment
IPM	Integrated Pest Management
IVM	Integrated Vector Management
LCD	Liter per Capita per Day
MDGs	Millennium Development Goals
NGO	Non Governmental Organization
PRSP	Poverty Reduction Strategy Paper
SIA	Strategic Impact Assessment
UNEP	United Nations Environment Programme
WHO	World Health Organization
WSSD	World Summit on Sustainable Development

Better management of the environment and wise investments in sustainable development are critical weapons in the battle against many of the world's most serious diseases, and essential interventions to ensuring health for all.

Dr Margaret Chan
Director General
World Health Organization

In recognizing the links between health and environment, we can motivate policy-makers to address the root causes of environmental degradation more assertively, preserve our planet's ecosystems, and ensure better health and well being for all peoples, in both developing and developed regions of the world.

Achim Steiner
Executive Director
United Nations Environment Programme (UNEP)

Acknowledgments

This report is the final product of the first phase of the WHO/UNEP Health and Environment Linkages Initiative, funded by Health Canada and Environment Canada.

In addition, the WHO/UNEP HELI Secretariat wishes to thank and express appreciation to all those individuals whose efforts made this synthesis report possible.

International steering committee

Geoff Barrett, Environment and Human Health Policy Division, Environment Canada, Ottawa.
Virginia Harel, Health Canada, Ottawa.
Bill Sonntag, United States Environmental Protection Agency, Washington DC.
Jan Huismans, United Nations Environment Programme (ex-officio), The Netherlands.
HNB Gopalan, United Nations Environment Programme (ex-officio), Nairobi.
Heinrich Wyes, United Nations Environment Programme, Nairobi.
Margaret Chan, Public Health and Environment (ex-officio), World Health Organization, Geneva.
Susanne Weber-Mosdorf, Sustainable Development and Healthy Environments, World Health Organization, Geneva.
Maria Neira, Public Health and Environment, World Health Organization, Geneva.
Maged Younes, Sustainable Development and Healthy Environments (ex-officio), World Health Organization, Geneva.
Hamed Bakir, WHO Regional Office for the Eastern Mediterranean, Regional Centre for Environmental Health Activities, Amman, Jordan.
Twisuk Punpeng, Department of Health, Ministry of Public Health, Bangkok, Thailand.
SK Mubbala, Coordinator, Ministry of Water, Lands and Environment, Kampala, Uganda.

Jordan country project

Hamed Bakir (coordinator), WHO Regional Office for the Eastern Mediterranean, Regional Centre for Environmental Health Activities, Amman.
Amer S. Jabarin, (team leader), University of Jordan, Amman.
Madi Tawfiq Al-Jaghbir, University of Jordan, Amman.
Saleh Malkawi, Ministry of Water and Irrigation, Amman.
Adel Belbeisi, Ministry of Health, Amman.
Kareman Al-Zein, Ministry of Health, Amman.
Ahmad Qatarneh, Ministry of Environment, Amman.
Eberhard M. Wissinger, Consultant, Ministry of Environment, Amman.
Munjed Al-Shareif, Jordan University of Science and Technology, Amman.
Jamal Ashour, Jordan University of Science and Technology, Amman.
Sireen Naoum, University of Jordan, Amman.
Raed Badwan, National Center for Agricultural Research and Technology Transfer, Amman.
Abdulfattah Jaljuli, WHO Regional Office for the Eastern Mediterranean, Regional Centre for Environmental Health Activities, Amman.

Thailand country project

Twisuk Punpeng (coordinator), Department of Health, Ministry of Public Health, Bangkok.
Theechat Boonyakarnkul (manager), Department of Health, Ministry of Public Health, Bangkok.
Nuntana Sabrum, Health System Research Institute (HSRI), Bangkok.
Duangjai Rungrojcharoenkit, Health System Research Institute (HSRI), Bangkok.
Navin Sopapum, Health System Research Institute (HSRI), Bangkok.
Jittima Rodsawad, Department of Health, Ministry of Public Health, Bangkok.
Plengsak Pookajorn, Department of Health, Ministry of Public Health, Bangkok.
Decharut Sukkamnued, Health System Research Institute (HSRI), Bangkok.
Sombat Haesakul, Health System Research Institute (HSRI), Bangkok.
Suphakij Nuntavorakarn, Health System Research Institute (HSRI), Bangkok.
Marut Jatiket, Thai Educational Foundation, Bangkok.
Kevin Kamp, SAFE Danida, Bangkok.
Hein Bijlmakers, IPM Danida, Bangkok.
Nussarapon Ketsomboon, Khon Kaen University, Khon Kaen.
Pattapong Ketsomboon, Khon Kaen University, Khon Kaen.
Wichien Kertsuk, Khon Kaen University, Khon Kaen.
Sukhum Wongaek, Department of Agriculture, Bangkok.
Sakda Sriniwet, Department of Agricultural Extension, Bangkok.
Anucha Ketcharoen, Kamphaeng Phet Rajabhat University.
Prarop Kunthawan, Kamphaeng Phet Agricultural Office.
Tung Tong Sub-district Community and the relevant officers.
Orapan Srisukwattana (editor), National Health System Reform Office (HSRO), Bangkok.

Uganda country project

SK Mubbala (coordinator), Ministry of Water, Lands and Environment, Kampala.
Teddy Tindamanyire, Ministry of Water, Lands and Environment, Kampala.
Edith Kateme-Kassaijja, Ministry of Water, Lands and Environment, Kampala.
David Mugabi, Ministry of Water, Lands and Environment, Kampala.
Bob Ogwang, National Environment Management Authority, Kampala.
Kitamireke Jackson, Department of Water Resources Development, Kampala.
Cornelius Kazoora, Sustainable Development Centre, Kampala.
R Erone, Government Analytical Laboratory, Kampala.
Nsubuga Emmanuel, Government Analytical Laboratory, Kampala.

Kyokwijuka Benon, Veterinary Public Health, Entebbe.
CS Rutebarika, Ministry of Agriculture, Animal Industry and Fisheries, Entebbe.
Sandra Mwebaze, Ministry of Agriculture, Animal Industry and Fisheries, Entebbe.
Joseph Okello-Onen, Livestock Health Research Institute, Tororo.
Agaba E Friday, Second Deputy Coordinator, Ministry of Health, Kampala.
Robert Odongo, Ministry of Health, Kampala.
Winyi Kaboyo, Ministry of Health, Kampala.
S Mulyoki, Occupational Health & Safety, MGL&SD, Kampala.
Collins Mwesigye, World Health Organization, Uganda Country Office, Kampala.
Boaz Keizire, Ministry of Agriculture, Animal Industry and Fisheries, Entebbe.
Kauta Nicholas, Deputy Coordinator, Ministry of Agriculture, Animal Industry and Fisheries, Entebbe.
Tom Mugisa, PMA Secretariat, Ministry of Agriculture, Animal Industry and Fisheries, Kampala.
Ahmed Nejjar, WHO Regional Office for Africa, Brazzaville, DRC, Democratic Republic of Congo.

Technical reports

Jeremy Richardson, United Nations Environment Programme, Geneva, Switzerland.
Elaine Fletcher, World Health Organization, Geneva.
Jonathan Mathers, Department of Public Health and Epidemiology, University of Birmingham, Birmingham, UK.
Clare Davenport, Department of Public Health and Epidemiology, University of Birmingham, Birmingham, UK.
Jayne Parry, Department of Public Health and Epidemiology, University of Birmingham, Birmingham, UK.
Anantha Kumar Duraiappah, International Institute for Sustainable Development, Winnipeg, Canada.
Paolo de Civita, Health Canada, Ottawa, Canada.
Thierry de Oliveira, United Nations Environment Programme, Nairobi.
Decharu Sukkumnoed, Health Systems Research Institute, Ministry of Public Health, Bangkok, Thailand.
Frank Ackerman, Tufts University, Medford, USA.
Sombat Heasakul, Health Systems Research Institute, Ministry of Public Health, Bangkok, Thailand.
Margaret Phillips, (Consultant), London, UK.

Advisers and reviewers

Pierre Quiblier, (HELI Secretariat) United Nations Environment Programme, Geneva.
Diarmid Campbell-Lendrum, (HELI Secretariat) World Health Organization, Geneva.
Annette Prüss-Üstün, World Health Organization, Geneva.
Carlos Corvalan, World Health Organization, Geneva.
Carlos Dora, World Health Organization, Geneva.
Jamie Bartram, World Health Organization, Geneva.
Robert Bos, World Health Organization, Geneva.
Eva Rehfuess, World Health Organization, Geneva.
Fiona Gore, World Health Organization, Geneva.
Bakary Kante, United Nations Environment Programme, Nairobi.
Halifa Drammeh, United Nations Environment Programme, Nairobi.
HNB Gopalan, United Nations Environment Programme (ex-officio), Nairobi.
Heinrich Wyes, United Nations Environment Programme, Nairobi.
Adnan Z Amin, United Nations Environment Programme, New York City, USA.
Maaike Jansen, United Nations Environment Programme, New York City, USA.
Hussein Abaza, United Nations Environment Programme, Geneva.
Monique Barbut, United Nations Environment Programme (ex-oficio), Paris.
Fulai Sheng, United Nations Environment Programme, Geneva.
Otto Simonett, UNEP/GRID-Arendal, Geneva.
Kevin Lyonette, Consultant, Geneva.
Dafina Dalbokova, WHO Regional Office for Europe, Bonn.
Michal Kryzanowski, WHO Regional Office for Europe, Bonn.
Fadi Doumani, Consultant, Washington, DC.
A. Sattar Yoosuf, WHO Regional Office for South-East Asia, Delhi.
A. Hildebrand, WHO Regional Office for South-East Asia, Delhi.
Hisashi Ogawa, WHO Regional Office for the Western Pacific, Manila.
Ahmed Nejjar, WHO Regional Office for Africa, Brazzaville, Democratic Republic of the Congo.
Lucien Manga, WHO Regional Office for Africa, Brazzaville, Democratic Republic of the Congo.

Editor and writer: Elaine Fletcher
Design and layout: Rob Barnes
Text editor: Jo Woodhead
Administrative support: Eileen Tawffik

TABLE OF CONTENTS

	PREFACE	9
	EXECUTIVE SUMMARY	11
I.	DEFINING THE LINKAGES	15
	1. Environmental hazards and health impacts	16
	2. Human settings and economic sectors	18
	3. Ecosystem frameworks for health and environment	18
	4. Focus on vulnerable populations	22
	5. Towards integrated packages of interventions for linked health and environment action	24
II.	IMPROVING HEALTH AND ENVIRONMENT DECISION-MAKING Challenges, needs and opportunities	25
	1. Drivers of health and environment decision-making	25
	2. Health and environment ministries: a closer look	27
	3. From data to decisions: using evidence effectively	29
	4. Bridging the evidence-to-policy gap	29
	5. Key needs of decision-makers: intersectoral dialogue; assessment and tools for quantifying health and economic impacts	30
	6. Engaging decision-makers and stakeholders	30
	7. Communication with decision-makers and stakeholders	31
III.	TOOLS FOR MANAGING HEALTH AND ENVIRONMENT LINKAGES Impact assessment: from evidence to decisions	33
	1. Current practice and problems in HIA and EIA	33
	2. Environmental impact assessment	34
	3. Health impact assessment	34
	4. Enabling conditions for effective impact assessment	35
IV.	QUANTIFYING IMPACTS IN HUMAN AND FINANCIAL TERMS Burden of disease assessment and economic valuation	37
	1. Quantifying population health impacts	37
	2. Making the economic case for health and the environment	38
	3. Challenges for economic assessment	41
	4. Relating economic valuation to policy-making	41

V. IMPROVING HEALTH AND ENVIRONMENT DECISION-MAKING 43
Guidance on integrated approaches

  1. Integrating health and environment impact assessment with economic development 43
  2. Guiding principles 43
  3. Defining the decision-making and assessment scenario 44
  4. Step by step process components 45

VI. THE PILOT PROJECTS 49
Jordan, Thailand and Uganda

  1. Jordan: water is life 50
  2. Thailand: reducing environmental risks and enhancing health through sustainable agriculture 58
  3. Uganda: livestock, ecosystems and development 71

VII. CONCLUSION 81
Consolidating health and environment linkages: a contribution to global policy agendas

  1. Reconciling fragmented approaches 81
  2. Repositioning health and environment sectors towards proactive policies 83
  3. Critical link to the achievement of global development priorities 83

REFERENCES 85

PREFACE

With a tragic series of extreme weather events and natural disasters, as well as the emergence or re-emergence of disease threats, recent history has been a harsh reminder of the critical linkages between human health and environmental conditions, as well as the long-term and immediate human, social and economic costs of ignoring these.

Some 60% of the world's vital ecosystems are degraded or being subjected to unsustainable pressures, concludes the recent Health Synthesis Report of the Millennium Ecosystem Assessment, a project involving 1300 scientists worldwide and UN agencies including the United Nations Environment Programme (UNEP) and World Health Organization (WHO). These 'services' refer to the complex biological mechanisms that sustain clean air, fertile soils and water resources for daily life, and provide us with the basics of food, fibre, fuels and medicines.

As we degrade our environmental benefits, we are lagging behind in providing the preventive public health strategies that we need to protect us against the resulting health risks. Potentially avoidable environmental risks currently cause almost a quarter of the total burden of disease. The greatest impacts are on children and other vulnerable populations in developing countries.

Demonstrating such linkages between health and environment is, however, only the first stage. The critical step is how we respond. Some of the threats can be addressed by the health or environment sectors acting alone, but many cannot. The complex and interlinked range of hazards and risks requires the development of integrated policies that address health, environment and development goals coherently. They should be founded upon up-to-date scientific knowledge, reliable assessment methods and good practice management tools that are accessible to decision-makers.

Such integration is sorely lacking. For too long, policies regarding environment, health and economic development have been designed in parallel, not in concert.

More integrated approaches require simultaneous action on multiple fronts including:

- a renewed moral commitment to sustainable development;
- political partnerships emphasizing proactive approaches to decision-making;
- technical solutions addressing root drivers of environmental degradation and resulting health risks upstream in the development process.

In response to the need for a more coherent policy agenda on health and environment, WHO and UNEP joined forces at the 2002 World Summit on Sustainable Development (WSSD) to launch the Health and Environment Linkages Initiative (HELI). Sponsored by the Government of Canada and supported by the United States Environmental Protection Agency, HELI was designed to translate scientific knowledge into policy action. As a product of the partnership spirit of Johannesburg, HELI provides a concrete example of effective cooperation between UN institutions at international, regional and country levels. It harnesses the comparative advantages and capacities of WHO and UNEP for a greater United Nations system coherence.

We believe that policy-makers from not only health and environment, but also a broad range of economic sectors, can draw both inspiration and technical direction from the resources contained in this synthesis report and tool kit. We hope that, like all partners involved in the process, they will share our conviction that it is only by addressing health and environment issues together that the real value of each can be appreciated fully, and incorporated into development agendas for enhanced human well-being.

HEALTH ENVIRONMENT

JEAN-LEO DUGAST / Still Pictures

A TOOLKIT FOR DECISION-MAKERS | 10

EXECUTIVE SUMMARY

The aim and scope of the Health and Environment Linkages Initiative

The initiative supports environment and health actors working together to address issues of common concern. Traditionally, health and environment sectors have acted independently of one another, each in defined domains. While much can and has been achieved, HELI aims to add a further dimension by focusing specifically on the large and important range of decisions which cannot be taken by one sector alone – and require a coordinated approach.

HELI aims to ensure that environment and health considerations are given their proper weight in decisions, particularly in the context of economic development. It is now broadly understood that decisions taken outside of the health and environment sectors – usually to promote economic development – often have the greatest effect on environment and health conditions. The HELI initiative aims to help health and environment sectors combine forces to proactively address shared areas of concern, e.g. promoting new energy or urban transport investments to tackle poor indoor and urban air quality. HELI aims to support health and environment sectors to engage in cross-sectoral dialogue, so that selected policy options achieve sustainable development objectives – enhancement of health and well-being, environmental protection and economic development.

HELI addresses targeted gaps in knowledge and tools needed for more effective integration of environment and health issues into decision-making. HELI's mandate, as defined at the 2002 World Summit on Sustainable Development, called upon the initiative to improve linkages between health and environment issues in science-to-policy forums, and particularly in the development context. Strategies for fulfilling this mandate were considered at a Needs Assessment Workshop in Cuernavaca, Mexico in 2003. There, participants identified key areas where the initiative should provide particular support and guidance to policy-makers. These areas included: improving linkages between health and environment impact assessment; linked economic valuation of health and environment impacts; and development of a knowledge base of policy-relevant resources. Strategic opportunities for the initiative to make a difference were further identified and refined in a global review of decision-makers' needs, conducted by HELI, and described in Chapter 2. The HELI initiative has been supervised by an International Steering Committee including HELI's original sponsors, Health Canada and Environment Canada; representatives of the Governments of Jordan, Thailand and Uganda; the US Environmental Protection Agency; and WHO and UNEP.

The initiative is designed primarily to inform the decision-making process rather than generate scientific knowledge. The assessment tools presented here are the result of a 'demand-driven' process responding to specific needs identified by decision-makers, particularly the need for better integration of health and environment priorities into development policies, and better management strategies to achieve that integration. At the same time, the focus on impact assessment and economic valuation is admittedly selective. Many other useful tools and procedures exist to assist decision-makers in prioritizing environmental health problems and to address those problems sectorally, as well as through cross-sectoral action. While not addressed in detail here, they are worthy of separate and detailed consideration.

This synthesis report highlights key findings of the initiative, and introduces a "tool-kit" to support integration of environment and health considerations into decision-making. The report represents the culmination of a two-year process of working with stakeholders to identify: current gaps in knowledge and tools that preclude better decisions; strategies for addressing those gaps; a clearinghouse of linked health and environment knowledge and resources; linked health and environment guidance on assessment procedures; and pilot-testing of the approaches in the field. Each chapter outlines a key theme, and refers the reader to detailed background reports and information sources available on the CD-ROM that accompanies the *Synthesis Report*, and on the WHO/UNEP HELI Clearinghouse. (www.who.int/heli)

Key findings and resources

Chapter I. Overview of Health and Environment Linkages

Poor environmental conditions cause a large proportion of the global burden of disease. Maintenance of environmental goods and services underpins all aspects of human health and well-being.

This chapter provides a brief outline of the ways in which health and environment linkages are typically defined and framed by policymakers – as a first step to understanding and prioritizing the problems they face, and shaping responses. Such linkage may range from a quantification of health impacts from a particular environmental hazard, (e.g. urban air pollution and premature mortality); examination of risks in particularly vulnerable populations (e.g. urban populations, children or workers); and examination of ecosystem-health linkages in specific settings (e.g. coastal, watersheds, or global). The chapter concludes that each framework is useful and complementary in different policy settings. All frameworks lead to the same basic conclusion: environmental goods and services underpin human health, and poor environmental conditions cause a significant proportion of the global burden of disease.

Chapter II. Improving Health and Environment Decision-Making: Challenges, Needs and Opportunities

Many of the ultimate drivers of environment and health conditions lie outside the direct jurisdiction of the relevant sectors. Environment and health actors need to increase their leverage on economic development decisions.

This chapter, the result of a global review of decision-making and interviews with key informants in a broad range of settings, describes the special institutional and political barriers encountered by health and environment policymakers in addressing the root drivers of environmental health risks. Economic development is regarded as being one of the major drivers of health and environment impacts, even if such impacts are often overlooked or ignored. The report documents the need for improved information and tools for intersectoral impact assessment of economic development policies and projects. Fora that promote engagement between policymakers, scientists and the general public also must be supported. Finally, the analysis underlines the importance of using improved communication and advocacy tools and strategies, to engage key actors across sectors and bridge the gap between scientists, the public and policymakers.

Chapter III. Tools for Managing Environment and Health Linkages

Policy choices could be improved through more systematic, transparent, and wide-ranging consideration of their impacts on environment and health.

Any time a policy is being considered, impacts are weighed, informally if not formally. This chapter reviews the formal impact assessment tools that have traditionally been used to evaluate the health and environment impacts of development and investment, including: environmental impact assessment, health impact assessment and newer forms of strategic, integrated and intersectoral assessment. The chapter concludes that formalized, mandatory impact assessment processes have their limits in term of feasibility and usefulness. Such impact assessment procedures can be inflexible and expensive. The evidence that they exert a major influence on health and environment decisions is inconclusive.

Oldrich Karasek / Still Pictures

Nonetheless, the principles that underline such impact assessment methods remain critical ingredients to any good decision – guiding a systematic consideration of how alternative policy options are likely to impact environment and health in a particular setting. HELI has thus sought to identify a flexible "menu of options" for good practice application of impact assessment. This menu aims to promote the assessment of linked health and environment impacts in a range of policy and decision-making forums, where health and environment need to coordinate with other actors.

This guidance may be particularly relevant to assesment of:

- Economic development and investment strategies identified by the health and environment sector as potential responses to an identified priority risk (e.g. energy investments to address indoor air pollution).

- Development strategies and investments originating in other sectors, but demanding a health and environment assessment/response due to the potential for impacts (e.g. a new transport infrastructure project with consequences for health and environment).

Chapter IV. Quantifying Impacts in Human and Financial Terms: Burden of Disease Assessment and Economic Valuation

Quantification of impacts of decisions in human and economic terms is a powerful tool to promote action and to improve decision-making.

Chapter IV highlights the importance of measuring the impacts of decisions in terms that resonate directly with policy makers. Impacts on health and impacts on the economy carry such resonance. Environmental burden of disease assessment provides a quantitative measure of impacts on health, providing a means for estimating morbidity and mortality in a given population, as a result of specific environmental risk factors, or in some cases, a particular policy or project. Full economic valuation of impacts on health, environment, and the economy is more difficult, but offers a distinct potential. Such assessment can provide a more comprehensive picture of the overall costs and benefits of decisions in a single monetary measure, easily understandable to policy makers, and readily comparable with alternative policies. This chapter also describes how burden of disease assessment and economic assessment have been used in real life settings to support sustainable policies, as well as fields where they are problematic.

Chapter V. Improving Health and Environment Decision-making: Guidance on Integrated Approaches

There is need for clearer and simpler guidance on integrating health and environment issues alongside economic considerations.

This guidance provides a rationale and approach to the conduct of 'linked' assessment of health and environment impacts, incorporating economic valuation into the method. Instances where such assessment approaches are likely to be more feasible and useful are cited – e.g. assessment of economic investments or development policies outside of direct health sector control. The aim of this guidance is *not* to create yet another set of guidelines for a highly formalized or statutory assessment process. Rather, the aim is to recommend key principles and strategies for assessment that should be integral to any policy dialogue. These include: involvement of relevant stakeholders in a transparent process; quantification and valuation of health and environment impacts where possible; and relevance of qualitative assessment and local knowledge. Such good practice guidance is relevant to decision-making in multiple fora and at multiple levels – from local policy decisions to broad national debates and more formalized impact assessment procedures with the heavier 5- or 10-step processes as usually defined.

Chapter VI. The Pilot Projects

Integrated health and environment approaches can work in the field.

The pilot projects describe the real-world experiences of three countries (Jordan, Thailand and Uganda) in testing linked health and environment decision-making approaches in the context of HELI. The assessments brought together, often for the first time, national policy-makers and experts in health, environment and other government sectors to carry out joint assessments and make joint policy recommendations, from an integrated health and environment perspective, and taking into account economic development needs and realities. In no case were these assessments part of a traditional mandatory or regulatory impact assessment procedure. Instead they aimed to shape existing and planned investments in key economic sectors in a manner that considered health, environment and economic synergies and tradeoffs together – rather than in isolation from each other.

The project in Jordan demonstrated that proposals to enhance water-resource management in the domestic and agricultural sectors would simultaneously create economic benefits in terms of water savings, environmental benefits in terms of reduced rates of aquifer depletion and reduced energy demand for water pumping, and health benefits from reduced rates of diarrhoea. A conservative economic analysis indicated that aggregated benefits would outweigh costs by more than 2.4:1.

In Thailand, an integrated health and environment impact assessment demonstrated how failure to manage the rapid increase in agrochemical use threatened biodiversity, health of farmers and consumers, and economic development, through risk of export bans. The project highlighted that the main constraint on use of healthier and more sustainable agriculture and pest control methods was largely related to poor management and dissemination of knowledge at the field level, rather than lack of scientific knowledge about good practice overall. The project catalyzed broad support for a comprehensive national programme to promote healthy agricultural strategies, (e.g. integrated pest management) which can reduce health and environment impacts, while sustaining agricultural development and farmer well-being.

In Uganda, the HELI project evaluated the health and environment impacts of policies promoting alternative modes of livestock management, a critical economic sector. The assessment indicated that very intensive commercial modes of livestock management may yield the largest gain in terms of short-term economic productivity. In contrast, somewhat less intensive and semi-mixed systems integrating livestock and crop production, or aspects of traditional agro-pastoralism, could offer substantial long term benefits for health, environment and economic development, as they reduce human exposures to chemicals used in livestock management and mitigate some of the risks of land and water degradation.

In each of the country projects, the focus on economically important sectors ensured that the project was considered relevant to national policy-making. The emphasis on economic valuation enhances understanding of the health and environment impacts of strategies undertaken in non-health sectors. The fact that environment and health agencies worked together from the start, and reached joint recommendations, gave greater coherence and weight to their findings.

Chapter VII. Conclusion: Consolidating Health and Environment Linkages

Environment and health partnership creates important synergies from local to national to international levels, and can make an important contribution to sustainable development.

HELI adds to the growing appreciation that integrated management of ecosystem services can yield not only health gains, but also significant economic savings, and therefore contribute to sustainable development. Such partnership also brings other benefits. Policy dialogue between health, environment and development sectors facilitates strategic cooperation in poverty reduction, as envisioned by the Millennium Development Goals and the WSSD Plan of Implementation. The remaining challenge is to ensure that such approaches can be replicated, refined and mainstreamed more broadly in the planning and processes of development agencies and country decision-making.

I. DEFINING THE LINKAGES
Frameworks and approaches

Interactions between environmental conditions and health impacts are characterized by multiple pathways of cause and effect. Policy actors and sectors tend to look at these multiple linkages through different lenses – each of which enhances a different aspect of the same basic set of problems. HELI has sought to relate to all of the major frameworks that are commonly used in order to stimulate thinking about more effective linked actions by health, environment and other sectors. These include the following frameworks.

- *Environmental hazards.* Environmental actors typically examine health and environment linkages through the lens of environmental hazards such as air and water pollution. This can help to identify policy responses such as monitoring of pollution emissions and mitigation strategies to reduce the pollution load.

- *Health impacts.* In the health sector, policies usually are focused on reducing a particular disease or group of diseases, e.g. vector- or water-borne. This can support policy responses ranging from health education for behavioural change to protective interventions such as insecticide-treated nets to control malaria.

- *Human settings and economic sectors.* Addressing problems in terms of human settings, e.g. urban, rural or occupational, often can help direct connection to the individuals that are most affected, and stimulate participatory action at the grass roots where it can have most effect. This can include personal and communal protection and prevention strategies as well as bottom-up initiatives to generate improved regulation, management and investment. Addressing issues in terms of particular economic sectors, e.g. water, energy, transport, agriculture, chemicals, or mining, can help advance mutually reinforcing policies, regulatory initiatives, voluntary programmes and investments for sustainable development.

- *Ecosystem approaches.* In recent years there has been a growing threat, not only from pollution at the local level but also from environmental stresses at the global level (e.g. ozone depletion and global climate change). In addressing these risks, it is often most useful to consider how natural ecosystems provide services to health such as clean water, food or protection from natural disasters. This can support improved management to protect or enhance ecosystem services, e.g. natural water purification capacity of watersheds; and reduce disservices, e.g. provision of vector-breeding sites.

- *Vulnerable populations.* Exposures and health risks from most environmental hazards are very unevenly distributed, often impacting most heavily on specific populations, including women, children, the poor or certain occupational groups. Appreciation of these vulnerable populations can help to target policy actions where they will have most effect in promoting health and health equity.

Using these frameworks as reference points, some of the most important patterns of health and environment linkages, hazards and risks of relevance to developing countries are presented below. Further resources on priority hazards and risks, as well as briefing papers, are provided more systematically in the HELI knowledge base and tool kit/CD-ROM and on line at www.who.int/heli.

HEALTH ENVIRONMENT

1. Environmental hazards and health impacts

Over the past decade, scientists have made significant progress in measuring the impacts of environmental hazards on human health. They have combined the best available monitoring data on levels of exposure to environmental risk factors with the results of epidemiological studies of their effects on various diseases to estimate the total burden of disease that results from environmental risks.

These linkages and impacts can be viewed through two lenses or perspectives, which are complementary:

- The lens of environmental risk factors i.e. asking how much disease is caused by a specific environmental hazard, such as indoor air pollution, and therefore highlighting the health gains that would result from addressing this factor.
- The "disease outcome" lens, by assessing the proportion of a particular disease that is caused by single or interacting environmental risk factors, such as the combined effects of land use, agricultural and water-resource management, and housing quality on vector-borne disease transmission. This can help to clarify the links for health sector workers whose activities usually are based around designing policies and programmes for specific diseases.

However they are viewed, the overall impacts are striking. From long-standing to emerging hazards, environmental factors are a root cause of an estimated one quarter of the global burden of disease – rising to more than one third in very poor regions such as sub-Saharan Africa (Smith, et al. 1999; WHO 2002; Prüss-Üstün and Corvalán 2006).

This body of work highlights the dramatic public health gains that could be realized through a preventive strategy that protects populations from major environmental hazards, and also promotes more sustainable investment and development strategies, natural resource management, pollution emissions control and land-use planning.

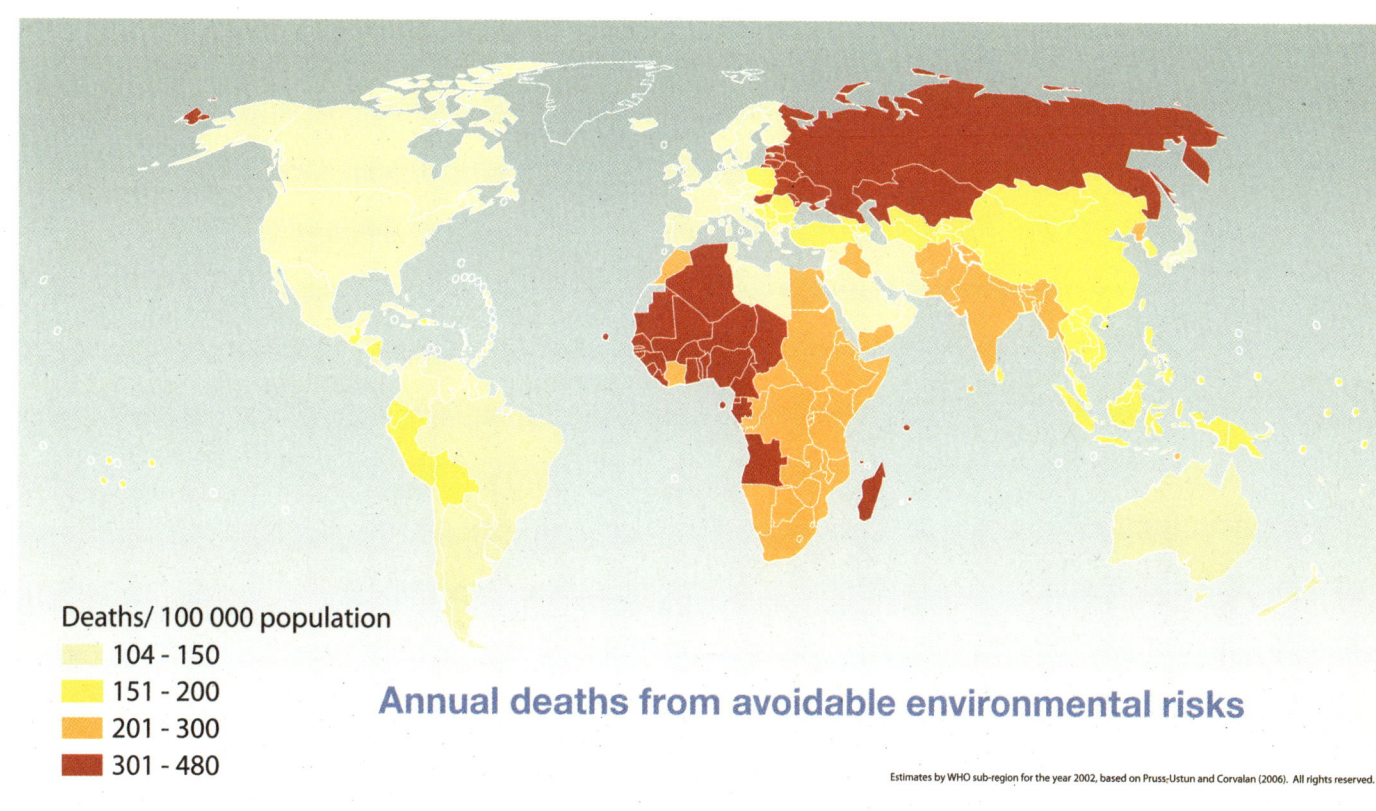

Deaths/ 100 000 population
- 104 - 150
- 151 - 200
- 201 - 300
- 301 - 480

Annual deaths from avoidable environmental risks

Estimates by WHO sub-region for the year 2002, based on Pruss-Ustun and Corvalan (2006). All rights reserved.

A TOOLKIT FOR DECISION-MAKERS

Burden of environmental disease

Major environmental risk factors with quantifiable disease impacts

- **Unsafe water and sanitation, poor hygiene.** This environmental hazard is estimated to kill nearly 1.7 million people annually largely as a result of a range of waterborne diseases, including diarrhoeal diseases.

- **Indoor air pollution.** Associated with solid fuel use, mostly in poor countries. Globally, 1.5 million people died from diseases caused by indoor air pollution in the year 2002.

- **Urban air pollution.** Estimated to kill about 800 000 every year. Elevated levels of fine particulates in ambient air – typically emitted by vehicles, industry and energy generation – are associated with increases in daily and long-term premature mortality due to cardiopulmonary diseases, acute respiratory infections and cancers.

- **Climate change.** Causes an estimated 150 000 excess deaths annually, as well as injuries, from more extreme weather events such as heatwaves, floods and droughts; impacts on regional food production; and changed transmission patterns of vector-borne and other infectious diseases.

- **Lead exposure.** Contributes to both childhood mental retardation and cardiovascular diseases associated with high blood pressure, together causing a loss of almost 13 million disability adjusted life years (DALYs - a combined measure of morbidity and premature mortality) annually, or nearly 1% of the global burden of disease.

For more information see:
- World Health Report 2002: *reducing risks, promoting health life* www.who.int/whr/en
- (Prüss-Ustun and Corvalan 2006) *Preventing disease through healthy environments* www.who.int/quantifying_ehimpacts/en
- *Quantifying environmental health impacts* www.who.int/heli/tools/en

Diseases with an important environmental contribution

- **Diarrhoeal diseases.** Some 94% of the 1.8 million annual deaths from diarrhoeal disease is attributable to environmental causes, particularly unsafe drinking-water and inadequate sanitation.

- **Lower respiratory infections.** Over 1.5 million deaths annually from lower respiratory infections (41% of the LRI disease burden) are attributable to environmental factors, largely associated with exposure to indoor smoke from solid fuels and outdoor (ambient) air pollution.

- **Vector-borne disease.** Over 500 000 deaths annually, or 42% of the global disease burden from malaria, are attributed to modifiable environmental factors such as poorly-designed irrigation and water systems; poor housing and settlement siting; deforestation and ecosystem change/degradation.

- **Road traffic injuries.** An estimated 467 000 deaths from road traffic injuries, or about 40% of the total annual disease burden from traffic injury, is attributable to environmental factors, e.g. transport and land-use designs that expose pedestrians and cyclists to excessive risks.

- **Unintentional poisonings.** Globally it is estimated that 71% of all unintentional poisonings, which kill about 350 000 people annually, are attributable to environmental factors. In developing countries, such poisonings are strongly associated with poor chemical management in agro-industries and occupational settings.

2. Human settings and economic sectors

Health and environment linkages also can be addressed more holistically in the context of human settings or economic sectors where multiple environmental hazards and health risks may exist, rather than through the lens of just one single factor. Consideration of environment-health linkages in particular settings – urban, rural or occupational – can aid examination of how certain hazards or risks interact with each other, e.g. poor waste-disposal practice, chemical contamination and water or air pollution. Settings-based approaches are particularly useful for actors which have responsibility for a specific location or population; e.g. they can help municipal authorities, community associations or trade unions to take action in addressing risks in their own homes, communities or workplaces.

While decision-makers such as mayors, local and regional councils, etc. are responsible for a very wide range of activities in a particular setting (e.g. a city, province or village), the majority of government decision-making functions, particularly at national level, are divided by sector, (eg. energy, transport, agriculture, health, industrial or water resource development). When large economic investments and major infrastructure projects are at stake, early consideration of all the health and environment impacts may be essential to minimize risks and optimize benefits. In many cases, relatively minor engineering solutions can have a major health impact if they are incorporated adequately into the initial stages of a strategy or development scheme – e.g. redesign of water-flow patterns in dams and irrigation schemes to discourage breeding of disease vectors, or the creation of pedestrian and cycle lanes in new road projects. National policies in water-resource management, agriculture and livestock management were the subject of particular focus in the HELI pilot projects (Chapter V).

3. Ecosystem frameworks for health and environment

The Millennium Ecosystem Assessment

Information is emerging constantly about not only the mounting risks to health from pollution and ecosystem degradation but also the positive contributions to health from ecosystem services.

Looking at health and environment linkages through an ecosystem framework captures a much broader web of interactions which is vital for good development decisions. Ecosystem services provide the essential plant and animal products for food, shelter, clothing and medicines. They purify and replenish air and water resources, ensure soil fertility, and provide leisure and cultural outlets. Other vital ecosystem services include biological systems of checks and balances that control many dangerous pathogens and disease vectors (e.g. mosquito vectors of malaria) and thus disease transmission, as well as regulating local and global climatic conditions.

The Millennium Ecosystem Assessment estimates that approximately 60% of Earth's major ecosystem services are being degraded or used unsustainably (WHO 2005; WRI 2005). The Health Synthesis Report notes the spectrum of health impacts that can result. Locally, contamination of water resources can exacerbate diarrhoeal diseases caused by lack of access to safe drinking-water. Global environmental changes can impact on agricultural production, exacerbating malnutrition, and spur more extreme weather conditions, causing injuries and deaths. The assessments conclude that pressures on ecosystem services will continue to grow in coming decades, with potentially serious implications for public health (WHO 2005a).

Policy solutions designed around ecosystem approaches may aim to repair, replicate or enhance the ecosystem services provided by nature – thus addressing multiple health and environment hazards and linkages simultaneously. For instance, improved coastal-zone management, orchestrated in a participatory manner by a community, may simultaneously support improved health and social well-being through improved social equity as well as a range of environmental goals, such as: fresh water quality in shallow coastal aquifers and streams; sustainable food production in marine waters; reduced breeding of disease-bearing vectors in wastewater pools, e.g. abandoned fish ponds; and the viability of natural sea and storm barriers, such as sand dunes, mangrove forests and coral reefs.

For more information see:
www.who.int/heli/risks/water/water/en/

Health and environment linkages

Occupational setting

Long-recognized hazards such as high levels of noise and dust exposure and excess burdens of toxic chemicals remain serious problems in many parts of the world. In addition to traditional occupational hazards, new cross-cutting health risks are emerging. These include health conditions associated with the use of new technologies, such as musculoskeletal conditions arising from exposure to machinery vibrations, as well as risks associated with subcontracted and informal labour arrangements, ranging from stress to unsafe working environments.

(Prüss-Üstün and Corvalán 2006) www.who.int/quantifying_ehimpacts/en

Transport

Unsustainable patterns of transport and urban land use are an often overlooked root cause of a number of significant and interrelated environment and health hazards, particularly in developing cities. Transport-related health impacts include the following.

- Urban air pollution. Particularly acute in developing cities.
- Road traffic injuries. Pedestrians and cyclists are among the most vulnerable groups. Environmental design of transport and land-use systems, including the lack of safe spaces for pedestrians and non-motorized vehicles, is a key risk factor (Peden, et al. 2004; Nantulya and Reich 2002).
- Physical inactivity. Patterns of urban land use and motorization are associated with sedentary lifestyles and the global surge in non-communicable diseases (Prüss-Üstün and Corvalán 2006).
- Inequalities. Access to health services is greater for those with vehicles than for those who do not, more often the poor.
- Community well-being. Transport is a driving force shaping patterns of social interaction, opportunities for physical activity, play and leisure.

www.who.int/heli/risks/urban/urbanenv/en/

Water sector

Water development policies designed to expand access to drinking-water, irrigated water for agriculture, or generate hydro-electric power, may impact on health both negatively and positively. These projects may improve food production capacity and increase the supply of available clean energy for cooking, heating and industry. At the same time, poorly-designed water, dam and irrigation systems may enhance the habitats of disease vectors such as mosquitoes that transmit malaria; disrupt natural hydrological ecosystems and natural water filtration processes; and exacerbate problems of water contamination from agricultural, industrial and human waste run-off. Conversely good ecosystem management of watersheds can yield health, environment and economic benefits.

www.who.int/heli/risks/water/water/en/

HEALTH ENVIRONMENT

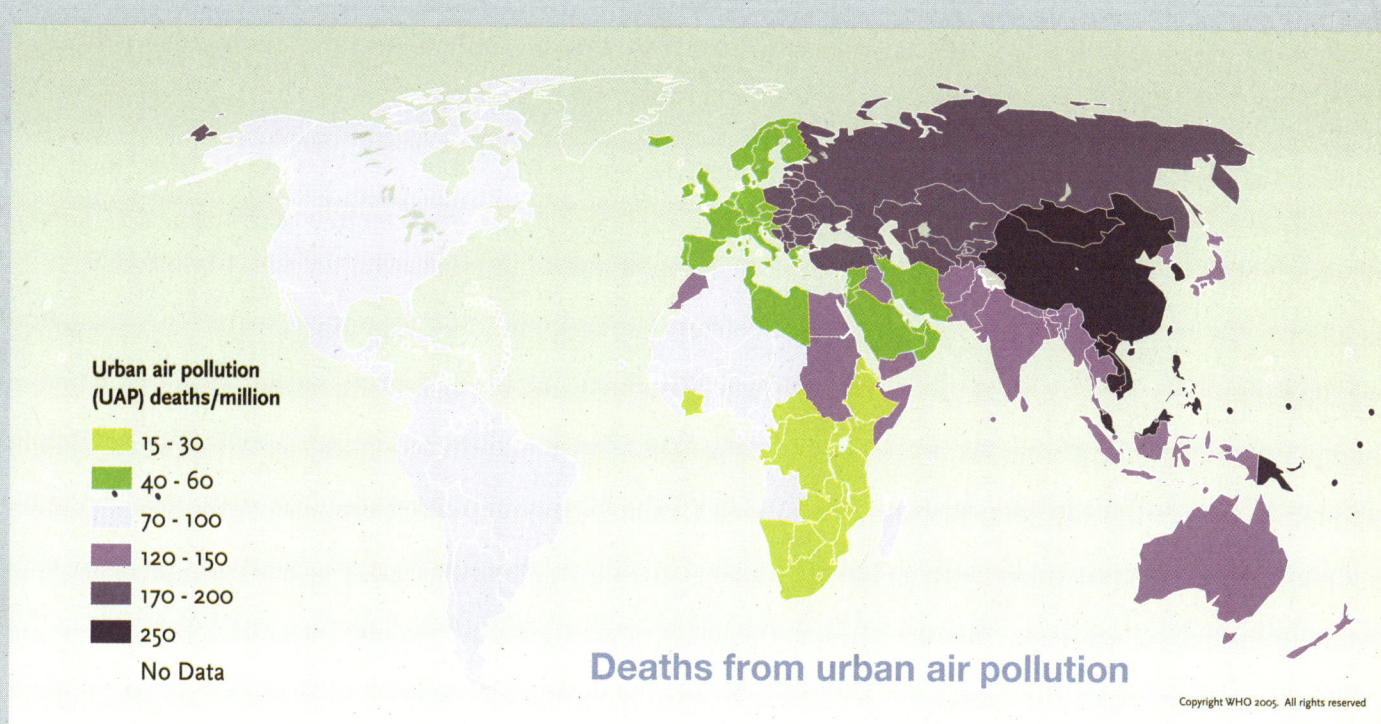

Deaths from urban air pollution

Urban air pollution (UAP) deaths/million
- 15 - 30
- 40 - 60
- 70 - 100
- 120 - 150
- 170 - 200
- 250
- No Data

Copyright WHO 2005. All rights reserved

Urban setting

Over the next 30 years, most of the world's population growth will occur in cities and towns of poor countries (UN 2003). Rapid, unplanned and unsustainable patterns of urban development are making developing cities focal points for many emerging environment and health hazards. As urban populations grow, the quality of the urban environment will play an increasingly important role in public health with respect to issues ranging from solid waste disposal, provision of safe water and sanitation, and injury prevention, to the interface between urban poverty, environment and health.

www.who.int/heli/risks/urban/urbanenv/en/

Energy sector

Indoor air pollution – generated largely by inefficient and poorly-ventilated stoves burning biomass fuels, such as wood, crop waste and dung, or coal – is responsible for the deaths of an estimated 1.5 million people annually. More than half of these deaths occur among children under five years of age. In developing countries with high mortality rates overall, indoor air pollution causes almost 4% of the total burden of disease.

According to current WHO estimates, more than half of the world's population cooks and heats with solid fuels, including biomass fuels and coal (WHO, 2006). Depending on how fuels are obtained and burnt, solid fuel dependency exacerbates deforestation, contributing to the build-up of greenhouse gases in the earth's atmosphere and thus to global climate change. Locally, deforestation can pollute streams with sediment and debris, generate soil erosion, loss of biodiversity and changed patterns of vector-borne disease transmission – all of which impact on health.

www.who.int/heli/risks/indoorair/indoorair/en/

A TOOLKIT FOR DECISION-MAKERS

Case studies of emerging and re-emerging diseases

Intact natural habitats keep many infectious agents in check. Conversely, global environmental changes and new patterns of human settlement and agricultural or livestock production, can lead to the emergence or re-emergence of certain diseases (UNEP 2005; WHO 2005). Deforestation, road and dam building and the expansion of cities can create the conditions in which new and old disease vectors may thrive. Poor handling of human and animal wastes; new forms of livestock production; related human-animal contacts and bushmeat consumption can facilitate transfer of pathogens from the natural environment to humans. Changed interactions between humans and wild and domestic animal populations are believed to have facilitated the emergence of BSE, avian flu, Nipah virus, SARS and AIDS as human health problems. Climate change also may aggravate the threat of certain infectious diseases. For example, the geographical range and seasonality of mosquito-borne infections, including malaria and dengue fever, are very sensitive to climate conditions (UNEP 2005) and are expected to shift as climate change progresses (Patz, et al. 2005).

Malaria

Deaths from malaria have remained steady or even increased slightly since 2000, reflecting the difficulties in reducing the disease burden, despite major international efforts (WHO 2004a). Malaria victims are overwhelmingly children and over 85% of malaria deaths, disease and disability occur in the African Region, with the South-East Asia and Eastern Mediterranean Regions second and third respectively.

Environmental conditions have a strong influence on malaria transmission in many locations. Deforestation and loss of biodiversity disrupt forest and river systems and may enhance the habitats for malaria-carrying mosquitoes. Other contributing factors are poorly-designed irrigation and water systems, inadequate housing, and poor waste disposal and water storage, which foster other common vector-borne diseases including leishmaniasis, schistosomiasis and dengue.

The large annual death toll from malaria and other vector-borne diseases, the development of vector resistance to some widely-used insecticides, and the costs of developing new treatments and insecticides and implementing insecticide-based control campaigns – all are indicators of the need for a more multifaceted approach to vector-borne disease. After several decades of reliance upon chemical forms of vector control, there is now renewed interest in also using environmental management tools to control malaria. This has been stimulated by new research demonstrating both the widespread efficacy of environmental management (Keiser, et al. 2005), and the fact that such techniques can be at least as cost effective as other disease control methods (Utzinger, et al. 2001).

www.who.int/heli/risks/vectors/malariacontrol

Dengue

Dengue fever, together with associated dengue haemorrhagic fever (DHF), has emerged or re-emerged in Asia, the Americas and elsewhere over the past three decades, and presently occurs in nearly 100 tropical and subtropical countries. Epidemics have become progressively larger: in 2002, the disease was responsible for an estimated 19 000 deaths and the loss of 616 000 DALYs (WHO 2004a).

Social and environmental factors – including increased urbanization (particularly of poor populations lacking basic health services) as well as expansion of international travel and trade – are linked to the resurgence of dengue. Lack of proper solid waste and wastewater management may be a factor as dengue vectors breed in standing water and discarded containers (Gubler 2004). Climate change also may affect transmission as dengue mosquitoes reproduce more quickly and bite more frequently at higher temperatures.

There is no curative treatment for dengue and space spray applications of insecticides have only a transient effect; more generalized community clean-up campaigns to remove breeding sites have proved difficult to sustain. However, more targeted environmental management strategies have been more successful: in south-east Asia, tiny crustaceans (copepods), natural predators of mosquito larvae, have been introduced to key breeding sites of the *Aedes* vector. These new experiences highlight how environmental management strategies, alongside improved health care provision and prevention, may provide a more effective package of interventions.

www.who.int/heli/risks/vectors/denguecontrol

Ecohealth: a transdisciplinary approach to health and environment linkages

Ecohealth approaches consider not only the physical environment and human interactions with ecosystems, but also various social, economic and cultural factors that can have a powerful range of impacts on both health and environment linkages. The Ecohealth framework, formally known as an Ecosystem Approach to Human Health, has been pioneered by the Canadian-based International Development Research Centre (IDRC).

Ecohealth frameworks are oriented towards action research and participatory research from a transdisciplinary perspective, using a broad and integrated conceptualization of ecosystems and human health. Ecohealth refers to not only the physical environment or physical disease conditions, but also health and environment linkages in a social, political and economic context. Human activities (or stressors) alter these contexts and have positive or negative effects on the individuals and communities involved.

The pillars of the approach are trandisciplinary investigation of these interactions; promotion of social and gender equity; and stakeholder participation. These are key to improving health and well-being as they are factors that catalyse change. Health promotion goes beyond personal lifestyle strategies to include more political and social issues, therefore policy, as well as personal and collective behaviour, are firmly the focus of attention. The approach recognizes the heterogeneity of communities and is especially attentive to vulnerable groups such as women, children, the elderly and other groups that may be socially, politically and economically disadvantaged.

EcoHealth frameworks typically have been research-oriented but research also should lead to communal and individual empowerment; new policy formulation; enhanced social and economic development processes, and improved interactions between scientists and society.

For more information see: www.idrc.ca/ecohealth

4. Focus on vulnerable populations

Children are among the main victims of environmental health risks. More than 4 million children aged 14 and under die every year from environmentally-related causes and conditions – out of an annual global toll of nearly 12 million (Prüss-Üstün and Corvalán 2006). Children are particularly vulnerable to vector-borne diseases such as malaria, and to diseases related to unsafe drinking-water and inadequate sanitation. Also they are heavily impacted by respiratory diseases related to indoor and outdoor air pollution. Childhood developmental characteristics and behaviour make children particularly vulnerable to unintentional injury, e.g. from road traffic, as well as to the acute and long-term health impacts of chemical exposures or acute poisonings. Children also bear the greatest burden of undernutrition and malnutrition, which in turn often is influenced by environmental factors such as the depletion of nutrients in soils; degradation of natural and agricultural ecosystems, climate variability and demographic pressures.

© Jareunsri -UNEP / Still Pictures

The health-environment-poverty link

The poor are more at risk from the health effects of both traditional and emerging forms of environmental pollution and degradation. Most of the world's poor still depend on solid fuels for cooking and heating, increasing the risk of respiratory illnesses from indoor smoke. Similarly, poor populations are more likely to be exposed to diseases associated with unsafe water and sanitation.

Poor agricultural and industrial workers, often working in the informal labour market or in substandard occupational health conditions, are at greater risk of acute poisoning and chronic illness from exposures to toxic substances, including pesticides and industrial chemicals.

The health impacts of climate change are likely to be borne disproportionately by poor populations, many of whom live in areas that are more vulnerable to the effects of a warming and more variable climate on weather-related natural disasters, including droughts, flooding and desertification.

Finally, the harmful effects of depleted ecosystem services are borne disproportionately by the poor, including indigenous populations, who rely more directly on ecosystem services for basic food needs, shelter, livelihoods and medicines, which are gradually being depleted by broader development processes (WHO 2005; DFID/EC/UNDP/WorldBank 2002).

Environmentally-related diseases not only affect the poor and vulnerable the most but also contribute to keeping them poor. Environmentally-linked illnesses and conditions have a direct impact on economic productivity, at both household and national level. Poor farm families affected by high rates of disease may shift to crops that may be less labour intensive but have a lower nutritional and/or cash value. Even after controlling for other factors, countries with intense malaria transmission had rates of GDP growth that were 1.3% lower than countries with less malaria, and countries with more than 50% of the population living at risk of malaria had average income levels that were one third of those in countries with less intense transmission (Sachs and Malaney 2002; Gallup and Sachs 2001).

5. Towards integrated packages of interventions for linked health and environment action

Clearly, health and environment linkages may be explored through multiple perspectives – each of which lends another, valuable dimension of understanding regarding driving forces and pressures, and health impacts.

Similarly, the most effective and efficient policies or strategies are likely to be packages of interventions that address linked health and environment problems along multiple points of interaction or multiple points in the chain of cause and effect. In technical terms, the key points to be addressed include the following:

- Improved ecosystem management that preserves or enhances positive ecosystem services that hold diseases in check, purify air and water resources, and replenish soils.
- Synergies between economic development, health and environmental strategies to optimize health and environment benefits, and minimize negative health and environment impacts from development.
- Effective control and disposal of pollution and waste emissions from industry, transport and all forms of human activity.
- Awareness, education and preventive health strategies to enhance personal protection and healthy behaviours in the face of environmental risks and hazards that cannot be eliminated completely (e.g. hand-washing, safe street crossing and protection from vectors).
- Broader reference to participatory processes, social, economic and gender conditions driving health and environment linkages.

Chapter II of this report explores more deeply the drivers of health and environment decision-making, and the barriers as well as the opportunities for promoting more integrated solutions.

Solar energy at an eco-tourism centre in Indonesia.

II. IMPROVING HEALTH AND ENVIRONMENT DECISION-MAKING
Challenges, needs and opportunities

There is basic knowledge about health and environment problems, even in settings with poor data and monitoring capacity. Scientific evidence, however, typically is just one competing factor in policy dialogue on issues impacting on environment and health.

In fact, the primary barriers to more effective policy are neither a lack of evidence nor a lack of knowledge. They are most often economic, institutional, political and social. That is the conclusion of the HELI review of Health and Environment Decision-making in Developing Countries, involving surveys of over 100 decision-makers globally and a wide-ranging literature review. Despite the barriers identified, significant entry points and opportunities do exist whereby scientific evidence may be introduced into policy dialogues, and policy-makers and the public may become engaged in more informed decision-making.

Improved interaction between science and policy-makers is critical to engagement strategies. Scientists are trained in dispassionate exploration of the physical world; scientific processes tend to analyse problems and phenomenon in small and discrete components, developing nuanced responses couched in probabilities. Policy-makers, as well as the public, tend to seek more absolute and holistic understandings related to people and their everyday problems. As a result, much compelling evidence on environment and health problems and impacts may not be communicated effectively.

To overcome these barriers, the "passion" of politics must be harnessed to the scientific "passion" for sound evidence and knowledge about the root causes of environmental degradation and related death and illness.

The HELI review focused on three levels of enquiry.

1. What are the driving forces in environment and health decision-making, particularly at the national and sub-national level?
2. What are the key barriers to more effective integration of health and environment evidence into decision-making processes?
3. What needs or entry points exist whereby scientific evidence on health and environment may be integrated more effectively into decision-making processes?

The review thus attempts to take a demand-driven approach to the issue of how scientific evidence might be used more effectively in decision-making.

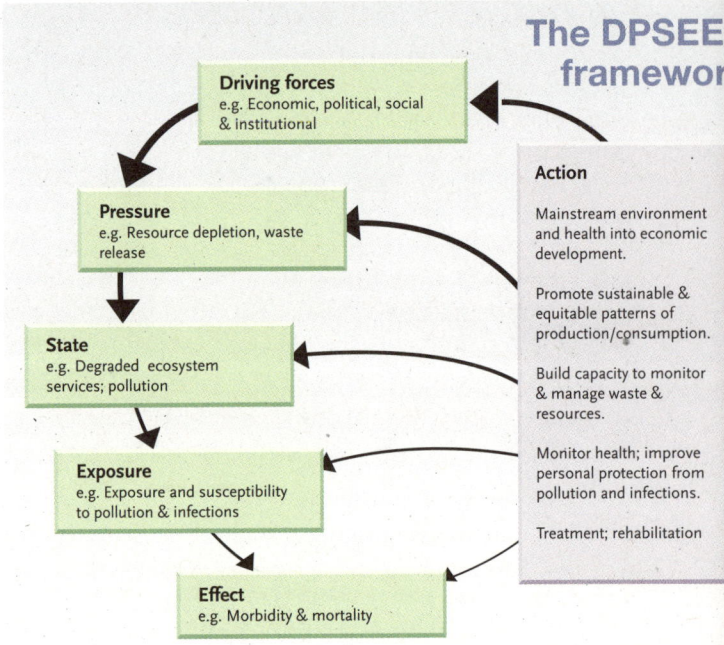

Adapted from Corvalán C, Briggs D, Zielhuis G., eds. (2000)

1. Drivers of health and environment decision-making

Economic and political drivers

Economic drivers, such as those listed below, are among the most powerful forces in decision-making globally. The development imperative shapes policy agendas directly and indirectly. The need to demonstrate short-term achievements in economic growth may override longer term considerations of resource sustainability, ecosystem degradation, pollution and ill-health.

- **Globalization of production, markets and trade.** Consumption patterns in wealthy countries drive pressures for unsustainable resource exploitation in poor countries, exerting pressures on traditional subsistence economies and natural ecosystems.
- **Market liberalization and structural adjustment policies.** In formerly state-controlled economies, liberalization may have weakened the public sector and thus

the capacity to manage environment and health risks effectively.

- **Political instability.** Shifting political rivalries; tribal and ethnic tensions; and – in the most extreme case – violence, may overshadow long-term national development goals.
- **Political alliances.** Economic, political and social interest groups may control and manage resources and production for short-term economic benefit, and generate excessive environment and health impacts.
- **Patterns of access to natural resources.** Inequitable allocation of natural resources may leave the poor little alternative but to exploit intensively those ecosystems and resources to which they do have access, exacerbating resource degradation and pollution.

Social drivers

- **Demographic pressures.** Most of the world's population growth over the next two decades will occur in developing countries, particularly around urban areas. Since the poor also rely more directly on natural resources for their livelihoods, pressures on natural resource bases and ecosystems may continue to increase. Urban environment infrastructures have not kept pace with the rapid rate of population growth in developing world cities, exacerbating urban health hazards from inadequate housing, sewage and transport systems.
- **Poverty barriers.** Particularly among the poor, daily survival is the all-consuming priority. It is important to link action on health and environment priorities with livelihood and well-being improvements, e.g. food security, new income generation and improvement of basic survival and well-being.
- **Awareness barriers.** The concrete link between common diseases and pollution or degradation may be displaced in time and space, and thus difficult to perceive. Disease and ill-health may be regarded fatalistically as an inevitable part of life, or a result of forces beyond human control.

Institutional drivers

The institutional context in which health and environment ministries operate is itself a driver of policy. Listed below are some of the institutional drivers of greatest relevance.

- **Pre-eminence of national and local agendas.** Although international policy agendas, including multilateral environment agreements, have relevance at critical moments, decision-makers must respond firstly to more local agendas, which may or may not place a high priority on environment and health.
- **Decentralization.** Over time, the widespread trend towards decentralization may improve government responsiveness to local environmental health issues, setting the stage for more participatory decision-making. Today, decentralized authorities often do not possess the technical, statutory and budgetary capacity effectively to collect, interpret and act on local health and environment evidence.
- **Sectoral divides between ministries.** Health ministries remain focused on curative health programmes. Environment ministries typically do not have direct jurisdiction over pollution emissions or natural resource management in key areas that influence health, e.g. transport, water resources or forests. Without inputs from health and environment, economic and development actors may not consider those impacts.
- **Donor and international/multilateral development priorities.** It is important that health and environment issues are integrated in donor priorities since donors may drive policy development in poor countries that are highly dependent on aid.

2. Health and environment ministries: a closer look

Health ministries and health professionals are focused on curative programmes, in terms of both professional formation and existing institutional structures. Environment ministries are generally newer and often more proactive in areas of legislation and regulation, but do not have health as an explicit focus. Also, in general, environment sector activities are not even as well-funded as budget-strapped health activities. While environmental expenditure is not reported systematically on a global level, available evidence indicates that environmental expenditure, as a proportion of GDP, often is far less than health expenditure.

In the health sector there has been extensive work to identify and cost per capita a basic basket of health interventions that can be promoted globally in developing countries. With no comparable formula for environmental health protection local decision-makers and managers have less concrete guidance on allocating resources for important environmental health investments.

Overall, blurred boundaries of responsibility for health and environment issues constitute a fundamental barrier to more effective decision-making. Responsibilities for environmental health may be divided between ministries and shift over time – falling between the cracks of institutional responsibility. Ministries generally tend to act most assertively on matters over which they wield explicit authority and most easily can obtain regular budget allocations or earn direct revenues. Institutional structures and financing mechanisms, as well as patterns of professional formation, thus fail to support intersectoral collaborations.

Harnessing synergies between health and environment

Environment and health issues will move higher on national agendas only through joint agendas, policies and actions. Despite the sectoral gaps and barriers, environment and health ministries possess complementary policy aims and professional skills. The environment sector has expertise in environmental pollution monitoring and regulation, while the health sector can relate environmental hazards to human health and well-being. Clear understanding of the mutual co-benefits to be gained from collaborative policy actions between health and environment sectors can provide at least an initial argument for greater cooperation. The real effectiveness of such an alliance, however, comes when the sectors work together to provide hard evidence that sound environmental management maximizes overall benefits to health, the environment and socio-economic development.

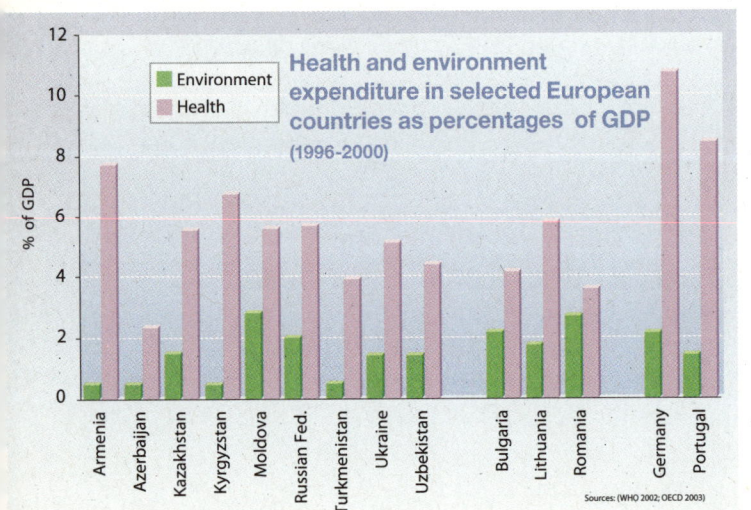

Health and environment expenditure in selected European countries as percentages of GDP (1996-2000)

Sources: (WHO 2002; OECD 2003)

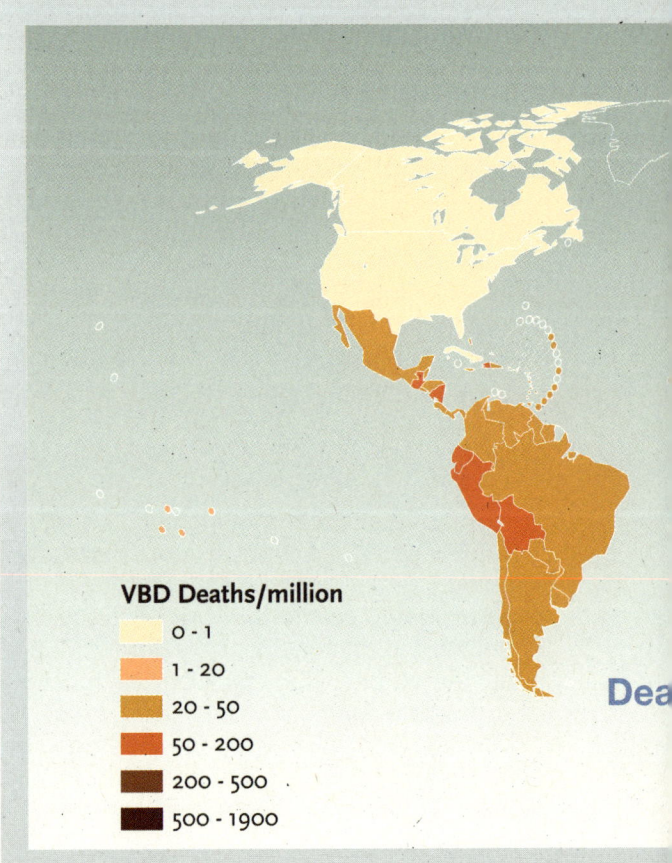

MANAGING THE LINKAGES FOR SUSTAINABLE DEVELOPMENT

Integrated vector management: the case for joint health and environment sector actions

New strategies for prevention and control of vector-borne diseases are emphasizing integrated vector management (IVM) – a multisectoral approach to vector-borne disease control that engages health and environment actors, as well as those in agriculture and water development.

IVM provides a framework for combining environmental management tools with improved personal protection strategies, along with accessible and affordable disease diagnosis and treatment. In many settings, use of IVM strategies has yielded sustainable reductions in disease and transmission rates, and supported more judicious use of insecticides via careful and targeted application, preserving their long-term efficacy and slowing the development of vector resistance.

Systematic review of the literature on environmental management and modification programmes has highlighted their effectiveness as malaria-control strategies (Keiser, et al. 2005). IVM field experiences also have been documented to be as cost-effective as other disease control measures, while also generating significant co-benefits to local economies in terms of development and growth (Utzinger, et al. 2001, Utzinger, et al. 2002).

IVM is only one example of how integrated management solutions, linking health and environment sector strategies, may provide a preferred menu of good practice interventions. Similar strategies exist to address other environmental hazards and health risks – such as integrated pest management (IPM); integrated transport demand management to address traffic injury risks and urban air pollution; and integrated water-resource management to address chemical and microbial hazards in water.

Each of these issues may be addressed jointly by health and environment sectors, together with development actors, at multiple points along the causal chain – from root cause to personal protective actions.

Examples of the application of IVM methods are described in detail in two policy papers available on the CD-ROM or on the website below:

- Malaria control, the power of integrated action
- Better environmental management for control of dengue.

www.who.int/heli/risks/vectors/vector/en

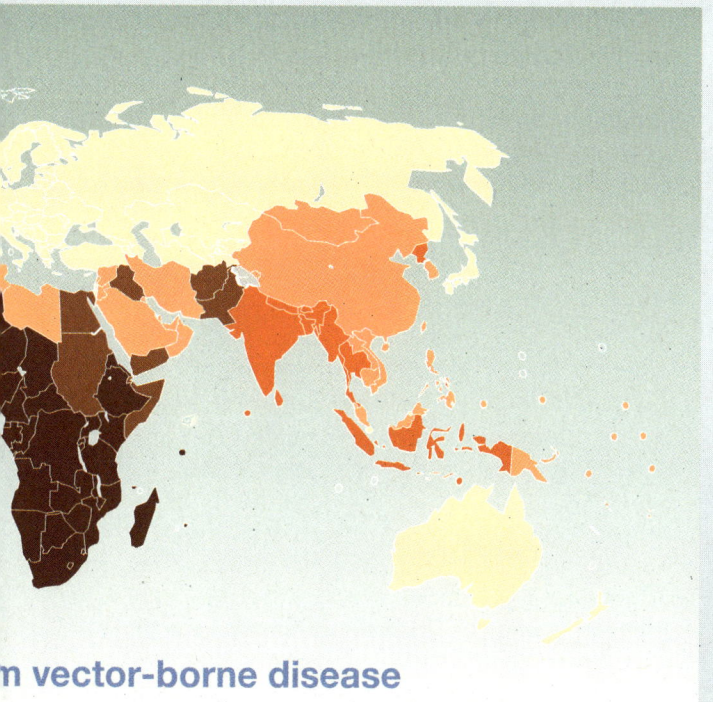

vector-borne disease

Estimates by WHO sub-region for 2002 (WHO World Health Report, 2004)
Copyright WHO 2005. All rights reserved.

3. From data to decisions: using evidence effectively

Lack of capacity to efficiently collect, synthesize and interpret technical health and environment data or indicators is cited as a continuing obstacle. However, problems may extend beyond staff or resource shortages, as detailed below.

- **Attitudes towards new technologies.** Data collected by new and unfamiliar technologies (e.g. satellite mappings of vegetation) in some settings may be viewed as less reliable than trusted expert opinion, and may not be used appropriately.
- **Political versus technical use of indicators.** Policy-makers may not refer to the same indicators as scientists. Political indicators of progress, e.g. symbols of social status or power, may be of great importance.
- **Weak impact assessment processes.** In many settings, impact assessment processes are technically weak or politically-driven, and thus ineffective as a policy lever. Usually health is not considered explicitly in environmental impact assessment, the most common tool.
- **Lack of familiarity with tools for quantifying health costs and benefits in human and economic terms.** Burden of disease and economic assessments are not used routinely. These tools can be extremely effective in describing impacts of policies in terms relevant to decision-makers: money and human lives.
- **Policy-to-practice gaps.** Policy assessment processes give insufficient consideration to what measures may be needed – in terms of economic incentives, regulatory action or voluntary campaigns – to support policy implementation, closing the gap between policy and actual practice.

4. Bridging the evidence-to-policy gap

Key informants regarded impact assessment as a powerful tool for incorporating evidence into policy considerations and processes. However, often this is not used effectively in many developing country settings. In particular, key informants stressed that impact assessments conducted at project level fail to influence more strategic decisions where the root drivers of health and environment risks could be addressed more effectively. It is essential to integrate impact assessment processes into strategic decision-making. The 55 countries of the United Nations Economic Commission for Europe (UNECE) recently adopted a provision for strategic environment assessment to build capacity in this dimension.

Informants regarded strategic, intersectoral or integrated forms of assessment also as more efficient, cost-effective and more likely to capture the full range of health and environment issues associated with particular development strategies or projects. In their opinions impact assessment processes that include components of monetary valuation of various health and environment benefits are more useful in communicating an economic "bottom line" to decision-makers. Such assessment processes and methods could be employed usefully in a variety of decision-making forums and channels, and not limited to statutory requirements. These issues are explored in Chapters III and IV.

Political versus scientific indicators: views of informants

"The lack of quantification and valuation of EH hazards prevents any dialogue on the issue. It's when you put a figure on the environmental health burden of disease that you can talk with decision-makers, especially the Ministry of Finance."

– Environment and health expert, World Bank

"The car is a status symbol everywhere and more so in developing countries. To own one shows you are successful. It is like wearing jewels..."

– Former Mayor, Bogotá, Colombia

"The main barriers to low-cost water solutions, for instance the renovation of traditional water sources with simple local materials, are the ones that relate to a politician's idea of status and visible progress. They would rather see a gleaming new hand pump, even if hundreds of hand pumps of the same sort have already been installed, were not maintained, and are no longer working."

– Water and sanitation expert, Zambia

"First and foremost it is imperative to illustrate how other countries elsewhere were able to overcome their problems. Start with successful policies, then provide burden of disease estimates, indicators & monitoring data, etc."

– Former Ministry of Health official, Ethiopia

5. Key needs of decision-makers: intersectoral dialogue, assessment and tools for quantifying health and economic impacts

Examination of the barriers to effective use of evidence leads to identification of the range of entry points for linking science to policy action, including those detailed below.

- Increased use of impact assessment intersectorally, not only in formal, statutory assessments of specific projects but also at the strategic level – for major infrastructure decisions, planning processes and poverty reduction strategies.
- Improved linkage of existing data on health and environment. Ideally based on local evidence, collected, synthesized and analysed with simple technologies, and presented in easily understandable units (such as economic impacts of burden of disease) for local decision-making processes.
- Improved linkage of impact assessment and economic valuation and analysis. Innovative methods of simple economic valuation, undertaken in consultation with stakeholders, can provide extremely useful input to decision-makers at very little expense (see box). Economic valuations should be linked directly to implementation plans, for example through infrastructure investments, regulation, tax and economic incentives.

6. Engaging decision-makers and stakeholders

Development of the scientific evidence base alone will not gain policy-makers' understanding and acceptance of evidence-based policies. For knowledge to be translated into policy, scientists, policy-makers and stakeholders need to be engaged in an interactive process of dialogue and change.

© Credit: Topham Picturepoint www.topfoto.co.uk

Successful engagement strategies generally are multifaceted, including interactive and outreach elements directly involving the targeted audience with the issue. Other important aspects of the engagement process include those listed below.

- **Potential solutions** should be presented alongside discussion of the problems to help overcome the sense of inertia and helplessness that decision-makers, and stakeholders, often feel in confronting environmental health issues.
- **Target explicitly barriers to change.** This requires neither confrontational strategies nor language, but honest exploration of how real problems may be surmounted.
- **Consider incremental changes.** Neither decision-makers nor their institutions are likely completely to discard long-entrenched attitudes and policies overnight.
- **Diversity of approaches to problems should be supported.** Grass-roots experience may be more important than theory. There is no one blueprint for success.

7. Communication with decision-makers and stakeholders

Effective communication strategies are the key to engagement and interaction between policy-makers and scientists. Generally scientists focus on developing a sound evidence base and may underestimate the challenges inherent in communicating that evidence to a non-scientific audience. The following communication strategies were identified as most useful and relevant.

- **Present case studies of good practice.** Discussion of the real experiences of others may be more convincing than abstractions; and successful applications more persuasive than evidence of the problems alone.
- **Reflect topical issues and priorities.** Identify how health and environment action also can advance other goals that are important to policy-makers and the public, such as job creation.
- **Present knowledge about health and environment in categories relevant to decision-makers and stakeholders.** At national level, health and environment issues usefully may be presented in terms of the sectors in which government ministries operate, e.g. agriculture, energy and transport. At local level, ecosystem or healthy settings' perspectives that relate more holistically to urban, rural, domestic and occupational environments may be very relevant.
- **Communicate in the language, forum and medium of decision-makers.** Terminology should be broadly understood – usually this is reflected in the terms and languages employed by local media. Briefings on key issues should be available at varied levels of detail for political and technical levels; web communication is most likely to reach professionals, academics and civil society groups rather than the top political echelon.
- **Communicate with rather than at the audience.** For instance, health workers who collect and examine mosquito larvae together with community members may be more effective in communicating messages about vector control. At the more technical level, distance learning via the Internet and "train-the-trainer approaches" used by farmer field schools, were cited as useful tools.
- **At grass roots, link environment and health problems to basic livelihood or survival issues.** Health and environment messages or measures that relate to these issues will be perceived as more relevant in very poor communities.
- **Sustained communications, 'marketing' and dissemination.** One-off campaigns are not enough. Messages are more effective when they are reintroduced gradually and reinforced over time. Sustained communications strategies and networking at global, regional and country level, signifies the kind of long-term commitment necessary to translate models to action.

For more information and full report see:
Fletcher E. *Health and environment decision-making in a developing country context.* Geneva, World Health Organization, 2008. www.who.int/heli/decisions/en/ .

HEALTH ENVIRONMENT

Advocacy plays a role in a water and solid waste disposal development project in Bhutan.

A TOOLKIT FOR DECISION-MAKERS

III. TOOLS FOR MANAGING HEALTH & ENVIRONMENT LINKAGES
Impact assessment: from evidence to decisions

Impact assessment, as formally defined, is the process of identifying the future consequences of a future or proposed action.[1] Whenever a policy decision is considered in a budget debate, cabinet decision or administrative policy, some generic assessment of impact – political, economic or social – is taking place. In this section we refer to impact assessment as any type of informal or formal consideration of impacts.

Some 30 years ago, the challenge of incorporating newly-recognized environmental issues into policy led to the development of formalized, step-by-step environmental impact assessment processes and methods. This formalized impact assessment offered a systematic procedure for gathering, analysing and presenting scientific knowledge, both qualitative and quantitative, to non-scientific forums of policy-makers and stakeholders, introducing evidence-related issues into policy debate.

Assessment processes have continued to evolve, in parallel with broader changes in policy-making strategies, to include these changes.

- A shift from specialist sectoral approaches to integrated approaches (e.g. environment and transport now tend to be treated in an integrated manner rather than as distinct policy areas). An integrated approach in policy preparation and implementation is essential for moving towards sustainable development.
- Moving from expert-led policy-making to approaches that embrace a range of stakeholder views and consider stakeholder perspectives and values.
- Moving from a rigid and prescribed policy preparation to processes based on a more flexible approach which is strong on outcomes but does not dictate means.
- Finally, shifting resources from the necessity of ensuring scientific certainty within the policy preparation process – sometimes characterized as "decide, announce and defend" – to processes that could be described as "implement, monitor and amend."

Impact assessment today includes methodologies with a sectoral focus, e.g. environmental or social, as well as broader processes such as strategic environmental assessment (SEA) and integrated or sustainability assessment. In an *ex ante* mode, impact assessment can identify the predictable costs, benefits, results and outcomes of the strategy, policy or programme whose adoption or implementation is under consideration – and it is at this stage that impact assessment may be of greatest value. Impact assessment also may be used in an *ex post* mode either to evaluate and adapt ongoing activities or to make a final analysis and evaluation of completed activities.

Approaches to impact assessment vary greatly according to the formality of the process; level in the policy and planning hierarchy; role of public participation; use of economic valuation techniques; and the balance of quantitative or qualitative methods used in analysis. However, to different degrees, all processes aim to predict impacts, involve stakeholders and influence decision-making (Davenport et al, 2006).

1. Current practice and problems in HIA and EIA

There is general agreement that systematic impact assessment processes can, in principle, support improved decision-making. However, the effectiveness of current approaches in achieving decisions that protect the environment and health is less clear.

The manner in which health and environment linkages are reflected in current impact assessment approaches was addressed at a HELI needs assessment workshop in 2003, convened in Cuernavaca Mexico; in the subsequent review of health and environment decision-making outlined in Chapter II; in a workshop convened at the 2004 conference of the International Association of Impact Assessment; and finally in two studies of health impact assessment (HIA) and environmental impact assessment (EIA) presented in this chapter. These HELI reviews identify how impact assessment processes are being used globally and how they might be used more effectively.

[1] *Impact assessment as defined by the International Association for Impact Assessment (www.iaia.org).*

2. Environmental impact assessment

Of the various impact assessment procedures relevant to environment and health linkages, EIAs are the most firmly established. Supported by well-defined procedures and guidelines, they have been applied for three to four decades throughout the world and are mandatory for many large projects. Potentially they are therefore a powerful tool for promoting and safeguarding human health from environmental risks. A literature review and series of interviews with specialists in the field identified key enabling conditions that can promote consideration of human health issues, many of which are applicable to all impact assessment processes (see below). Practitioners and users, however, also identified a series of commonly recognized problems and limitations on current EIA practice.

- Although strategic environmental assessments are becoming more common in developed countries, most environmental assessments are more limited, focusing on specific projects.
- Legislation for EIA is now in place in many developing countries, but local ownership of such processes can be weak – particularly as many EIAs are undertaken due to the requirements of outside (e.g. donor) agencies.
- The independence of an impact assessment process can be jeopardized if a government has a weak capacity to issue strong terms of reference, monitor the process and review findings.
- Often there is inadequate expert review of the quality of EIA reports and no post-approval follow-up and review of the implemented recommendations or requirements.
- If government and civil society review of impact assessment is weak, political pressures may override serious review of issues, particularly in cases where the assessment is financed by the project developer.
- In general, health is not well covered in present-day EIA processes. EIA is more likely to involve environmental experts rather than human health experts, leading to a lack of guidance, capacity or interest in evaluating health effects. This usually leads to health being treated as a sub-component of environmental impacts or ignored completely.

3. Health impact assessment

HIA applies the same basic principles as those applied in other impact assessments, but addresses human health considerations specifically. An international literature review commissioned by HELI showed that HIA is increasingly popular in developed country settings and is now beginning to be applied in the developing world, notably in south-east Asian countries such as Thailand.

This stock-taking provides important information on the application of HIA at this early stage of development. Most HIAs are applied locally and sectorally: of the 88 HIAs reviewed in the study, over 70% were undertaken at local or regional levels (63/88), 50% were tied to specific projects rather than more strategic programmes or policies. Transport and housing are the two most common sectors for application of HIA – probably because there is more scientific evidence linking these sectors directly to health outcomes, compared to others such as regeneration, land-use or agriculture.

Most HIAs considered in the review were initiated by non-governmental service and civil society organizations, often with expert input from academia or consultancies. The majority of HIAs were not proactive, but instead aimed to modify an existing or proposed project. Most strikingly, as yet there is little analysis of whether the HIA process actually influenced decision-making, or what features make an HIA successful or unsuccessful as a lever on decisions.

How did the HIA influence the decision-making process?

Was the HIA considered in the decision-making process?	Yes No Unknown	13 1 74
Did the HIA impact on the decision-making process?	Yes No Unknown	8 1 79

The analysis reflects factors that constrain the effectiveness of HIA as it is currently practised. Key constraints include a focus on local, project-based issues and a tendency for impact assessment to be applied to modify project proposals, rather than in the design phase. More fundamentally, much of the available guidance on HIA focuses on methodological issues (e.g. which data to use, reviewing the evidence, how to work with stakeholders). Most strikingly, prior to the HELI assessments, there had been little analysis of whether the HIA process actually influenced decision-making, or what features make an HIA successful or unsuccessful as a lever on decisions.

4. Enabling conditions for effective impact assessment

Experiences around the world generally identify the following key enabling conditions for effective impact assessment.

- Political commitment, especially from the higher levels of government, as well as clear mandates for the institutions conducting and/or reviewing the assessment and making policy recommendations.
- A sound legal framework to ensure that the impact assessment is applied systematically in all relevant situations.
- Early initiation so that findings can influence the policy, strategy or plan under review.
- Capacity-building, especially in developing countries, to build expertise in techniques and approaches to impact assessment, as well as in the development of effective terms of reference, review and monitoring.

Most fundamentally, impact assessment approaches need to ensure that the health and environment issues they highlight are taken fully into account in final decisions i.e. combined with other considerations such as the drive for short-term economic growth. Integrated assessment approaches, such as those conducted by UNEP in the developing countries of Africa, Asia and Latin America, potentially offer such a conceptual framework. This series of integrated assessments examined the economic, social and environmental impacts of trade and economic policies in sectors such as agriculture, fisheries and forestry.

However, health was not a primary focus of the analysis. A related tool, sustainability assessment, was modelled in central America by the Macroeconomics Programme of WWF-International in the mid-1990s to link local conservation initiatives with larger politico-economic decisions. A new protocol for the conduct of SEA of major policies, plans and projects, recently adopted by the United Nations Economic Commission for Europe, includes an explicit provision for health assessment but implementation is yet to be tested.

Integrated assessments also may be presented as economic analyses in which health, environment and other impacts are converted into monetary value, allowing calculation of overall measures of costs versus benefits.

Although useful in many situations, formal integrated assessments may not necessarily always be the most effective or the only way to support informed policy-making. If poorly designed or applied, they can lead to health and environment considerations being neglected, misrepresented or ignored. Research on impact assessment indicates that there is no one ideal approach. Different methods will suit different policy- and decision-making situations depending upon the sector; degree of integration sought; information available; level of detail required; culture of accountability and participation; range of options; and availability of time and resources.

Ultimately, maintaining the vision of what impact assessment is trying to achieve is more important than the process. Impact assessments need to provide a forum for effective and representative dialogue with stakeholders. Also they need to incorporate quantitative scientific data and qualitative information on health and environmental impacts to present it in a manner that decision-makers can understand and weigh alongside other considerations, such as economic costs and benefits. Finally, they need to be robust enough to absorb and withstand political pressures, maintaining independence while meeting the needs of policy-makers and planners.

HEALTH ENVIRONMENT

Maximizing the effect of impact assessment

- **Emphasis on participatory processes.** Stakeholder inputs improve transparency and ownership of results.

- **Burden of disease and economic valuation of costs and benefits.** Human health impacts summarized in quantifiable values provide powerful and easily-understood evidence to policy-makers about tradeoffs, choices and risks.

- **Integration of qualitative evidence with quantitative measures.** Locally-gathered qualitative and social evidence may add dimensions not captured in data, and may be critical where data are missing.

- **Diversity of approaches.** Recognition that there is no single road map for assessment supports the right of country-level decision-makers to tailor their approach to local needs.

- **Consideration of policy alternatives and implementation.** From the outset, assessment should consider policy alternatives so that root health and environment drivers are addressed. When recommendations are made, assessment should consider measures realistically to support policy implementation, e.g. economic, voluntary, etc.

For more information and full report see:

Mathers J, Davenport C, Parry, J. *Health impact assessment, Review and guidance on use of IA methodologies for including environment and health considerations into decision-making in a range of sectors,* Geneva, World Health Organization, 2006.

Richardson, J. *Environmental impact assessment: Review of impact assessment methodologies.* Geneva, World Health Organization, 2006.

www.who.int/heli/impacts/en/

Monitoring climate change to assess environment and health impacts, Burkina Faso.

A TOOLKIT FOR DECISION-MAKERS

IV. QUANTIFYING IMPACTS IN HUMAN AND FINANCIAL TERMS
Burden of disease assessment and economic valuation

Most development strategies involve health and environment trade-offs, even if they are not often recognized and valued. For example, building irrigation channels to provide a reliable flow of water may increase crop yields and incomes, but also may increase the incidence of diseases such as malaria, resulting in lost worker productivity and medical care costs. The majority of the economic benefits from increased crop yields may accrue to one group; increased disease-incidence may affect the same group – or an entirely different population altogether.

Simply describing these linkages is often not enough to ensure that they are given the required attention when policy decisions are made. Decision-making can be made more transparent and more responsive to stakeholders concerns when the consequences can be quantified in terms that relate directly to people's lives. There has been important progress in this field in recent years, with development of methods for measuring, ranking and comparing effects in two important dimensions: (i) human health; and (ii) economic costs and benefits.

1. Quantifying population health impacts

The most comprehensive approach to quantifying health impacts of environmental risk factors is through environmental burden of disease (EBD) assessment, developed by WHO. This combines the best available evidence on levels of exposure to the environmental risk factor, the association between the risk factor and specific health outcomes, and the level of those diseases in the population. This allows estimation of the burden of disease caused by the risk factor, usually given in terms of attributable deaths or DALYs for the population as a whole and, in some cases, for specific subgroups. The assessments therefore can give an easily understood "bottom-line" measurement of the overall health impact of a risk factor, and can show which sections of the population are carrying more or less of that burden. Under certain conditions it can also help to assess the health implications of projects or policies. For example, urban transport policies can be assessed in terms of their health impacts from changes in exposure to air pollution, and potentially via other causal pathways, such as through environmental noise.

While the box below summarizing steps in EBD methods is based on assessment of exposure combined with health data based on the best available evidence, it is also possible to systematically evaluate the impact of projects on the basis of a literature review combined with expert consultation. An example of such an approach is provided in Prüss-Ustün & Corvalan 2006.

WHO has now developed methods for estimation of health impacts from a series of environmental modifications (e.g. indoor and outdoor air pollution). Once the main parameters are known, the estimation of health impacts can be completed with relatively little effort, time and resources.

Environmental burden of disease

This aims to provide a quantitative measurement of the overall health impacts of an environmental hazard in a given population. It includes the following steps.

- Specify the health risk to be addressed.
- Specify the measure of exposure and the range of exposure to be considered.
- Derive the population exposure distribution.
- Select appropriate health outcome(s) to be considered (e.g. deaths, disease, injuries or DALYs which represent a weighted combination of the first three).
- Estimate exposure-response relationship in the population of interest, or derived from the scientific literature.
- Combine exposure and exposure-response relationship data for each population group under consideration (e.g. by age and gender).
- Calculate the number of attributable cases, or an attributable fraction of cases, multiplied by the health statistics associated with the disease(s) under study.
- Quantify uncertainty of the estimate (range of potential effect).

Such assessments should be consistent with other information on health and environment that is available for the study area. For example, the number of cases attributable to an environmental risk factor should be consistent with the total number of cases in a given population, and the presence of other risk factors for the same disease.

EBD assessments have three main advantages.

- Provide a single measure that combines all of the various health effects of a particular risk factor, to show the overall size of the problem.
- Results can be compared across risk factors and across populations, helping to identify which risk factors deserve greatest attention (e.g. showing whether a population suffers a greater disease burden from poor water and sanitation or from outdoor air pollution), and to highlight populations that are particularly vulnerable (e.g. showing that indoor air pollution from use of solid fuels causes disproportionate impacts on women, children and the poor).
- Can be applied not only to measure the impact of risk factors, but also to derive policy options to tackle them. They are therefore an important component of cost-benefit or cost-effectiveness analysis (below).

Quantitative assessment:
Web-accessible resources and tools

- Quantification of population health impacts (environmental burden of disease) assessment: detailed guidance at www.who.int/quantifying_ehimpacts/en/

- Quantification of population health impacts (burden of disease) assessment, policy brief: HELI CD-ROM/tool kit or www.who.int/heli/tools/en/.

- Scientific data and environmental health indicators: www.who.int/heli/tools/en/

2. Making the economic case for health and the environment

Identifying and measuring environmental health impacts can often gain the attention of policy-makers. However, actions to address these impacts involve resources – from the direct financial costs of interventions, to negative or positive effects on economic development.

HELI brought together a team of environment, health and economics experts to review current practices in economic valuation of the health benefits and costs of policy choices that impact upon the environment and ecosystem services. The economic analysis proposed in this paper provides a taxonomy of economic methodologies and instruments which can be used to address health-environment links; and a systematic approach to identify the economically most efficient and equitable policy intervention strategy and integrate it within larger development and poverty reduction strategies.

Getting the best deal: identifying economically efficient interventions

One of the most important criteria that policy-makers consider when choosing strategic interventions is the cost and benefit profile of

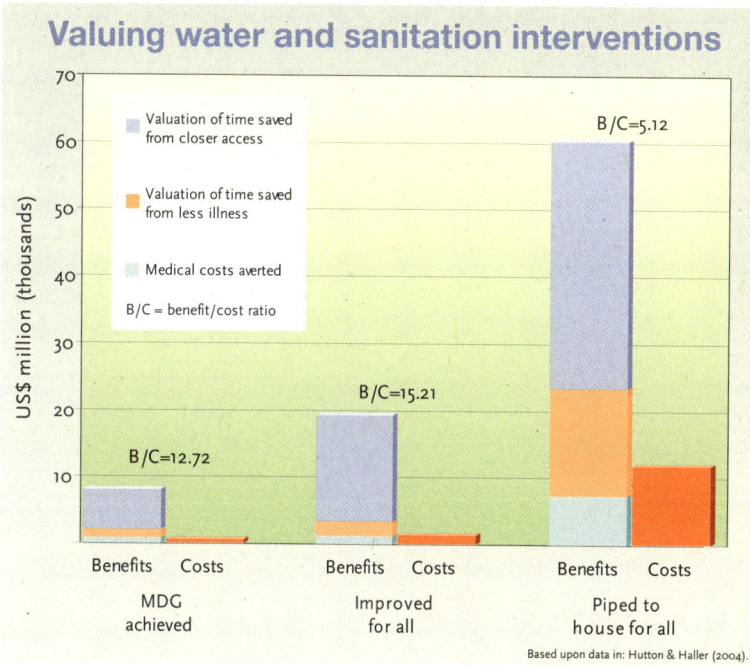

Based upon data in: Hutton & Haller (2004).

various options. Economic analysis helps decision-makers measure efficiency; either by reaching a defined health and environment goal with the lowest financial cost or by obtaining the greatest level of benefits from a defined level of resources.

Two main techniques are used to evaluate the economic efficiency of proposed strategies.

Cost-benefit (or benefit-cost) analysis is the most complete version of an economic efficiency analysis. It aims to calculate all of the health, environment and other benefits and costs resulting from a decision, convert them into a common (usually financial) measure and compare them against one another. The most common unit of measurement is the benefit-cost ratio which describes the monetary or welfare benefit per unit of currency spent.

Evaluation of the costs of actions can range from relatively simple measures: for example, the direct costs of simple environmental interventions based on similar programmes in the past, to more sophisticated models that include the costs of the financial, institutional and other transactions needed to carry out the intervention.

Estimating the benefits of the policy often is even more challenging, analytically and because valuing health and environmental impacts in monetary terms is sensitive and controversial. Since health and environmental quality are not usually bought and sold directly, specific market prices for valuing changes in these measures are not available. Usually, these are valued indirectly using either stated preference methods (i.e. how much people say they would be willing to pay for a particular benefit, such as a year of healthy life) or revealed preference methods (i.e. using people's actions, such as how much they pay for safer technologies). When primary research on the localized benefits of a policy is not available or feasible, the benefit transfer technique (using valuation measures from similar situations elsewhere) increasingly is employed.

Well-designed benefit-cost analysis can be a powerful tool, giving a clear message about whether the benefits of an intervention are likely to outweigh the costs from a societal perspective, and helping to choose the most efficient of alternative options. However, their usefulness depends on whether the full range of costs and benefits are represented accurately, and whether their valuation in the model (e.g. monetary value of health costs; environmental losses) is both transparent and based upon the best available scientific evidence.

Cost-effectiveness analysis (CEA) is a simplified benefit cost analysis often used today in specific sectors, such as the health sector. Benefits often are measured in terms such as the number of deaths or illnesses avoided, tons of emissions prevented or meeting a specified standard – without necessarily converting them into a monetary value. Some of these analyses (sometimes referred to as cost-utility analyses) use aggregate measures of "utility" as an outcome. These include summary measures of population health, which combine premature death and time lived with illness into a single measure, such as DALYs. The common unit of measurement is the cost-effectiveness ratio or cost-utility ratio, which describes health effect (e.g. cases averted or disability-adjusted life-years averted) per unit of currency spent.

The main advantage of the different kinds of cost-effectiveness analyses is that they avoid having to assign a monetary value to human health, environmental protection and other non-market goods. This makes them very useful when considering policy options that are limited to a single sector and that are likely to result in only a single or limited range of outcomes, e.g. medical interventions that directly affect specific diseases. Their major disadvantage is that the outcomes are not expressed in a common currency and so cannot produce a single bottom-line measure for decisions with a very wide range of effects (e.g. interventions that have major effects on human health, the environment and economic development).

Making fair decisions: analysing the distributive impacts of responses

The most cost-effective strategy is not always best for all, some groups may be worse off. There is a possibility that the best-case option according to economic efficiency criteria may have higher distributive costs than some of the other intervention strategies considered.

Equity effectiveness analysis is used to evaluate the distributive impacts of a policy on different social groups especially the poor and the vulnerable. Equity assessments are particularly important if the distribution of a policy's costs or benefits across different socioeconomic groups is likely to be uneven. Analysis should focus on the geographical and temporal distribution of effects (e.g. are the effects likely to be concentrated in a particular neighbourhood, community, or even countries in the case of global environmental changes? Are they likely to be greater for future generations?) as well as the distribution across key demographic variables such as income, ethnicity, age or gender.

Case studies of economic valuation of health and environment linkages

Regional and national level
When New York City was faced with a potential US$ 8 billion cost for building water filtration plants to comply with a new federal safe drinking-water act implemented in the 1980s, it set about examining more affordable options. In the mid-1990s, a new watershed protection programme was adopted in the Catskill watershed, which supplies most of the city's drinking-water, at a much lower cost of about US$ 507 million. Investment in improved watershed protection, through management of land use and agricultural, waste and storm water run-off, was deemed more cost-beneficial than creation of drinking-water purification plants. Extensive land-use, waste and water management plans were put in place to restore and preserve watershed purification capacity (USEPA 2005). Benefits of that approach are now being evaluated.

The HELI pilot project in Jordan projected the anticipated health and environment benefits that might be captured by accelerating investments in water efficiency, particularly to halt water leakage. Such analysis was based upon the associations between water stress and diarrhoeal incidence. On that basis, investments in improved water efficiency were estimated to be beneficial by a benefit to cost ratio of 2.4:1 (see Chapter VI).

Grass roots
In Thailand, farmers have used rapid economic valuation methods to assess the direct benefits and costs of adopting more sustainable agricultural practices such as integrated pest management. In Uganda, a participatory approach to valuation of the health benefits expected from sanitation improvements has been piloted in communities where WHO-supported health teams and local leaders together made rapid estimates of households' economic costs from sanitation-related diseases, e.g. diarrhoea. The analysis, in a lunchtime seminar, prompted local leaders to assign greater priority to sanitation improvements. Such methods have the potential to be more useful to local decision-makers in certain situations than highly formalized valuations costing far more money and time (see Chapter VI).

3. Challenges for economic assessment

The basic purpose of economic analysis is to help identify appropriate (efficient and equitable) choices and document the trade-offs in different approaches. In this way it can be a powerful tool in evaluating the health and environment implications of decisions.

Yet some of the apparent strengths of economic analysis can become weaknesses. Simple bottom-line assessments of whether costs outweigh benefits may be attractive and easy to understand, but this very simplicity can obscure important information. Final measures depend, for example, on the framing of the assessment (e.g. range of intervention options considered; costs and benefits included) and assumptions about the time course of the policy and its effects. Simple cost-benefit ratios also can obscure the distribution of costs and benefits within an affected population. These issues are particularly important when considering environment and health linkages where policies can have multiple long-term effects and those who benefit may not be those bearing the costs.

It is vital therefore that economic analyses in this field follow good practice in both execution and presentation of results, including the following considerations.

- Consider all relevant alternative options.
- Be transparent about the process by which impacts are quantified and valued, particularly in the case of multi-sectoral interventions with multiple potential impacts.
- Measure, value and discount costs and benefits using best available methods and evidence. When full quantification of a policy's potential impacts (favourable or unfavourable) is not possible, the analysis should present any relevant quantitative information and describe the unquantifiable or unvalued impacts, including the nature, timing, likelihood and possible distribution of such effects. A summary table will make it easier for decision-makers to integrate such impacts into their overall assessment.
- Identify industries, regions and social groups most likely to experience significant impacts (distribution and equity assessment).
- Take account of uncertainty. All economic analysis needs to deal with uncertainty resulting from inadequate data, limitations in the underlying science, limitations in the valuation of benefits and unpredictability of future conditions. In some instances, the degree of uncertainty can be reduced by gathering better data or improving the scientific understanding of key issues. In general, however, policy evaluations are conducted with imperfect information and analytical tools. Key areas of uncertainty can be explored through various forms of sensitivity analysis. In any case, the analysis should avoid suggesting a degree of precision that the current state of knowledge cannot support.

4. Relating economic valuation to policy-making

Economic analysis should not be considered the panacea for all problems. It can be very demanding in terms of data requirements, time, expertise and technology including economic models. But this is not a reason for abandoning the task altogether – economic analysis is not all or nothing. It can range from a simple evaluation of a number of discrete options to a substantial exercise involving months of fieldwork and the development of sophisticated quantitative models. The following have been identified as some features of an economic analysis that contribute to its effectiveness in influencing policy.

- A study with results that can be defended is more likely to be taken notice of. Good data and analysis are crucial.
- The economic analysis should explain thoroughly the methods and models employed and their embedded assumptions. They should note explicitly the key uncertainties and describe their effect on the overall conclusions.

- Results should be presented unambiguously – clear conclusions, use of appropriate statistical and graphic means.
- Even the most rigorous economic assessments are likely to be subject to important limitations and uncertainties. The results are therefore unlikely, in and of themselves, to justify a particular policy choice. Decision-makers will always need to take account of the broader policy context, legislative mandates and a host of other considerations that influence policy development. The more the result of the analysis is situated in this broader context the more helpful it will be to decision-makers.
- Involve key stakeholders depending on the scale of the assessment, for example: relevant government ministries, departments and representative NGOs for national strategic assessments; key representatives and individuals for community-level decisions.
- Consider mechanisms not only to evaluate alternative options but also to ensure that they are implemented. This can include using economic analysis to support and design economic tools such as pollution taxes that translate health and environment externalities into user charges and promote innovation to reduce environmental damage.
- Integrate economic analysis of health and environmental effects' key planning processes that determine economic development, such as poverty reduction strategies.

The ultimate test of such economic analysis, however, is not whether it produces a high benefit-cost ratio, but whether it supports policy changes that enhance ecosystem services to well-being in an equitable manner, over the long term. There is a need for further field-testing of these approaches (particularly in developing countries), followed by monitoring, consideration of lessons learnt and refinement of the methods, to make them as effective as possible in supporting sustainable development.

For more information and full report see:

Duraiappah AK, de Civita P, de Oliveira T, Sukkumnoed D, et al. *An economic approach for evaluating health-environment linkages*, December 2004, WHO/UNEP Health and Environment Linkages Initiative, Geneva. www.who.int/heli/economics/en/

Guidance on issues to consider in evaluation of cost-effectiveness of environmental health interventions is presented on the website, *Quantifying environmental health impacts*:
www.who.int/quantifying_ehimpacts/cost_effectiveness/en/

Guidance on economic and cost-effectiveness issues with regards to water, sanitation and health is presented at Water, health and economics on the WHO web site: *Water, health and economics*.
www.who.int/water_sanitation_health/economic/en/

Guidance for conducting cost-effectiveness of health interventions is available on the WHO website: Choosing interventions that are cost-effective (CHOICE).
www.who.int/choice/en/

V. IMPROVING HEALTH AND ENVIRONMENT DECISION-MAKING
Guidance on integrated approaches

HELI focuses on improving the decision-making process. This chapter outlines general principles and components of a process to integrate the best available scientific knowledge on environment and health linkages, along with the values and perspectives of those affected, and brings them to the attention of those responsible for taking decisions.

An important focus is to assist policy-makers in government and civil society, particularly in developing countries, to mainstream environment and health linkages into the preparation and implementation of policies, budgets, plans and programmes. Given the intimate interaction between health, environment and poverty, integration also can support the preparation of poverty reduction strategy papers (PRSPs) and other forms of national development plans that are more cost effective and beneficial for sustainable development.

The guidance therefore outlines a process for impact assessment in the broad sense, as a management tool for assessing the full range of consequences of a particular decision. While such an assessment should produce a scientifically-valuable outcome, the utility of assessment and scope in which it can be used goes beyond the boundaries of pure science, and should contribute to the implementation of "best practice."

This guidance represents an initial synthesis of international experience and good practice arising from the review and survey work undertaken in HELI, as well as pilot project assessment experiences with country partners. Intersectoral cooperation was identified as of prime importance, and three key needs were identified to promote greater intersectoral cooperation.

1. Integrated impact assessment tools and processes linking health and environment assessment.
2. Integration of qualitative and quantitative methods, particularly burden of disease and economic valuation.
3. An environment which encourages and facilitates exchange, participation and interaction between scientists, policy-makers and stakeholders.

1. Integrating health and environment impact assessment with economic development

Uni-sectoral assessments may produce accurate and useful conclusions within the limits of that specific sector. However, given the powerful linkages and causal relationships between health and environment, considerable advantages can be achieved by looking at these together. Most notably, good environmental management promotes good health and averts the need for certain types of investment in public health, saving scarce financial resources for other uses. Particularly in developing countries, the links between these two sectors should be acknowledged and the synergies between the two exploited – through more unified policies, integrated operations and the considerable economies that can be achieved in delivering health plus environmental outcomes.

To be taken seriously in the decision-making process, however, health and environment considerations must also be grounded in economic realities. Advances in epidemiological analysis, which have permitted more accurate quantification of the human burden of disease from particular policies, also have led to the development of techniques for economic quantification of the health and environmental impacts of policies. While further work is needed, these methods are already being used in consideration of health and environment policies in developed countries and could be highly relevant to developing countries where efficient use of economic and natural resources is even more critical.

2. Guiding principles

Certain key concepts are essential to carrying out a successful integrated assessment.

- The integrated approach in no way downgrades or substitutes for the value and relevance of the best available scientific expertise within a specific sector, such as health, the environment or economics. On the contrary, it attempts to provide a framework within which the best available specialist information can have the maximum effect in improving decisions.

- A multisectoral integrated assessment is, of necessity, a blend of quantitative and qualitative scientific analysis and of validation through the dynamic process of stakeholder input, participation and dialogue. These should not be handled as separate stages of activity but rather as an ongoing, interactive relationship generating, sharing and using mutually useful information.

- The success or failure of a policy depends, among other factors, on the consensus and sense of ownership among the affected community. Local participation can improve the quality of the analysis, design and implementation of any intervention. More importantly, it leaves in place local capacity that can continue and develop the process over time.

The following sections outline a series of steps that aim to ensure a comprehensive treatment of the issues in a progressive and inclusive process. Throughout the assessment process the basic approaches, criteria and principles need to be adapted to the specific circumstances of the assessment and to the capacity and resources available.

3. Defining the decision-making and assessment scenario

Due to its dynamic and participatory nature, the various scientific and process components of a multisectoral integrated assessment must be regarded as of equal importance and each must be carefully structured, implemented and blended. Such integrated assessments are likely to use both quantitative and qualitative methods of data gathering and analysis, depending largely on the nature of the data available and on the stakeholder concerns and priorities (see graphic below).

DECISION ENHANCING
Early assessment assists in the preparation of policy evaluation of options and has wider organisational learning benefits

1. Learning and Scientific

3. Learning and Deliberative

←**QUANTITATIVE**─────────────────────**QUALITATIVE**→
Technical assessment including quantitative baseline data

Participatory and deliberative techniques for evaluating significance

1. Evaluative and Scientific

3. Evaluative and Deliberative

DECISION LEGITIMISING
Assessment of preferred option to identify positive and negative as well as mitigate unacceptable effects impacts and casts

Measuring water quality to assess health impact.

It is inevitable that according to local demands and needs, some assessments will have a greater emphasis on scientific evaluation of options while others will concentrate more on deliberation and enhancing local capacity and learning.

4. Step by step process components

Throughout the assessment process, there is a range of choices to be made about the precise orientation of the assessment, e.g. deliberative or scientific; expected outcome; range of stakeholders; range of scoping; depth of sectoral survey; use of indicators; methods of valuation and data gathering. At the same time, following the sequence of steps outlined below can help to ensure comprehensive treatment of the issues in a progressive and inclusive process.

a. Identifying priority issues to be addressed

This initial "scoping" phase aims to define the issues to be assessed taking into account the purpose of the policy or practice under assessment, the expected output of the process and the available capacity, methods and resources (human, temporal and financial). Focus and precision are basic to a good assessment. The most efficient way to carry out the initial definition of the issues to be addressed is often for a small group representing the most obviously affected sectors (e.g. ministries of environment, health and planning) to produce an initial proposal for a priority issue to be addressed.

The primary justification for carrying out an integrated assessment is that the issue should lie at the intersection between health, environment and development rather than obviously within one or other sector. Other important criteria are strong evidence for significant impacts on the natural ecosystem, human health and livelihoods, including evidence of current or potential future burden of disease; and urgency, either because the issue is coming to a crisis or tipping point, or because a proposed action, or inaction, is likely to have long-lasting or permanent effects.

b. Forming an interdisciplinary core group

Few decision-makers, technical experts, or members of the public are familiar with integrated assessment. It is therefore important to define a working structure that brings people into the process, and applies their skills as efficiently as possible. The best way to achieve this is often by first setting up a "core group" of technical experts, whose work is then reviewed and commented on by a more inclusive stakeholder group.

The core group should ideally be composed of experts from health, environment and economics. It is important to incorporate, as early as possible, institutions that have direct technical expertise, and also those that will be directly involved in funding and implementing the decision. For example, if the issues for assessment are related to public policy and expenditure, it would be helpful if the team includes an economist from the development or public expenditure "stream" of economics, since they will often be responsible for taking the final decision on the use of public funds.

While each expert must retain the quality of her/his specialist knowledge, each must also be committed to participate in an approach where specialist knowledge is shared within the team and thus is enhanced by benefiting from, and contributing to, the quality of the cumulative and collective output.

c. Ensuring stakeholder participation

Participation and dialogue with a wider range of stakeholders is equally important to the process. They constitute a "reality check" of the technical and scientific analysis. For this reason, the term stakeholder should be interpreted in a broad and inclusive way.

- Government ministries (development, finance, planning and treasury among others) will incorporate outcomes into policy and practice.
- The private sector, which has major potential for driving positive change.
- Local communities, who will have to live with the results of any policy decision.
- Civil society organizations such as NGOs, community and professional associations.

Often it is very useful for the core team to attempt to map out and define the institutional or economic profile of stakeholders and actors in relation to the assessment issues: Who plays a major role? What is their motivation? Who can be a strong advocate for positive change? Who has the resources or influence to make a difference? How do, and how should, the major players interact? What capacity for change exists or could be promoted?

Interaction between the core group and wider stakeholders should not be a one-off activity, but should be started early, and continued at key points through the duration of the assessment. The most critical points are during the initial scoping phase to ensure the assessment captures key concerns, during the assessment to ensure that local expertise and perspectives are utilized, and at the end, to ensure that the recommendations have a wide endorsement and a mandate for implementation.

d. Defining the linkages, identifying policy options

Describing the links between the drivers of environmental states and conditions, their effects on health exposures, and ultimately on the health of human populations, is the basis for identifying action points for improved health and environment decisions.

Various approaches exist for mapping out these links. These include frameworks defined by the Millennium Ecosystem Assessment and by UNEP, which focus on the linkages between environmental conditions, ecosystem services and human well-being. They also include the DPSEEA (Driver, Pressure, State, Exposure, Effect, and Action) framework, which has a greater focus on health outcomes themselves.

Each of these approaches can be useful in placing the issue within its wider context, and making clear the full range of actions that can help to improve conditions, including influencing "upstream" drivers. This focus on identifying and evaluating interventions is a crucial distinction between a purely research-driven exercise and policy assessment to improve decision-making.

It is important to consider the wide range of potential interventions that could be implemented, either on their own or in combination. These include economic incentives, technological interventions, social measures such as health promotion, and legal or regulatory measures. Obviously, responses must be compatible with local priorities, institutional structures and capacity. Focusing on policies that are either in development or already "on the table" can help to ensure that the assessment is relevant to local needs.

HIA exercise in south east Asia

Road works in the Amazon: how do health and environment benefits and costs in the transport sector add up?

e. Assessing the options, sector-by-sector

The first stage in assessing policy options is for the various experts to use their specialist skills to contribute the most comprehensive and scientifically sound assessment of the likely effects of policies within their own sector. This can include a variety of methods, such as using burden of disease methods to consider the overall effect of alternative policies on human health; ecological assessment with reference to key indicators, e.g. loss of forests, loss of cultivated land, pollution emissions, to measure impacts on the environment; and livelihood and poverty assessments to consider impacts on human well-being. Both quantitative and qualitative methods will almost always be needed, but the emphasis will vary according to the context and aim of each assessment.

f. Putting the pieces together

The final step of the purely scientific assessment phase is to compare the likely impacts of each response strategy directly against one another.

Economic valuation can be a crucial tool in providing a single "bottom-line" measure to assist policy-makers to understand and act on the outcomes of the assessment. Ideally, this consists of a full cost-benefit analysis valuing all health, environment and environment externalities, as well as direct and indirect compliance, institutional, social welfare and transitional costs. It should also include a socioeconomic analysis to reveal the distributional aspects of the benefits and costs of the identified responses.

In practice, however, cost-benefit analyses are rarely truly comprehensive, as complete and accurate data on all costs and benefits are difficult to obtain. It is therefore essential to highlight gaps and possible biases in the assessment, and to use qualitative information to fill these gaps and provide guidance in interpreting the results.

The process and conclusions also need to be shared with, and reviewed by, the stakeholder group to verify their appropriateness and accuracy and incorporate additional data or analytical input. This meeting also can address the proposed financing mechanisms for implementing policy recommendations.

g. Communication and delivery of results

Assessment results must be made intelligible to the broad audience involved in any development process. This includes decision-makers, government officials, NGO leaderships, representatives of local organizations and private enterprises, and civil society in general. Three factors are important determinants of success (i) the level of clarity with which complex results and relationships can be presented (ii) linking the presentation to topical debates concerning development, health and environment (iii) how well the presentation's starting point takes account of the levels of knowledge and awareness of the topic among different groups of actors and audiences.

Engagement and communication

- The media can make an important contribution both as stakeholders and deliverers of conclusions.
- The stakeholder group's own media potential should be exploited fully – officials, research institutes, the private sector and NGOs have their own established means of contact with the media and the public.
- It can be extremely effective to have a local champion – a person who enjoys wide public recognition and respect and whose involvement in the delivery process automatically will command attention.
- Meetings and briefings for selected groups (Chambers of Commerce, professional associations) and the interested general public, can raise media awareness and support for the policy recommendations.
- Training courses and briefings for fellow professionals in universities, research institutes and schools can help mainstream the recognition of the linkages and interdependence between health and environment and establish capacity to monitor, evaluate and iterate the process.

For more information and full report see:

Lyonette K, Campbell-Lendrum D, Quiblier P. *Guidance for integrating health and environment impact assessment incorporating economic valuation*, Geneva, United Nations Environment Programme/World Health Organization, 2006.

www.who.int/heli/impacts/en/ and

www.who.int/heli/economics/en/

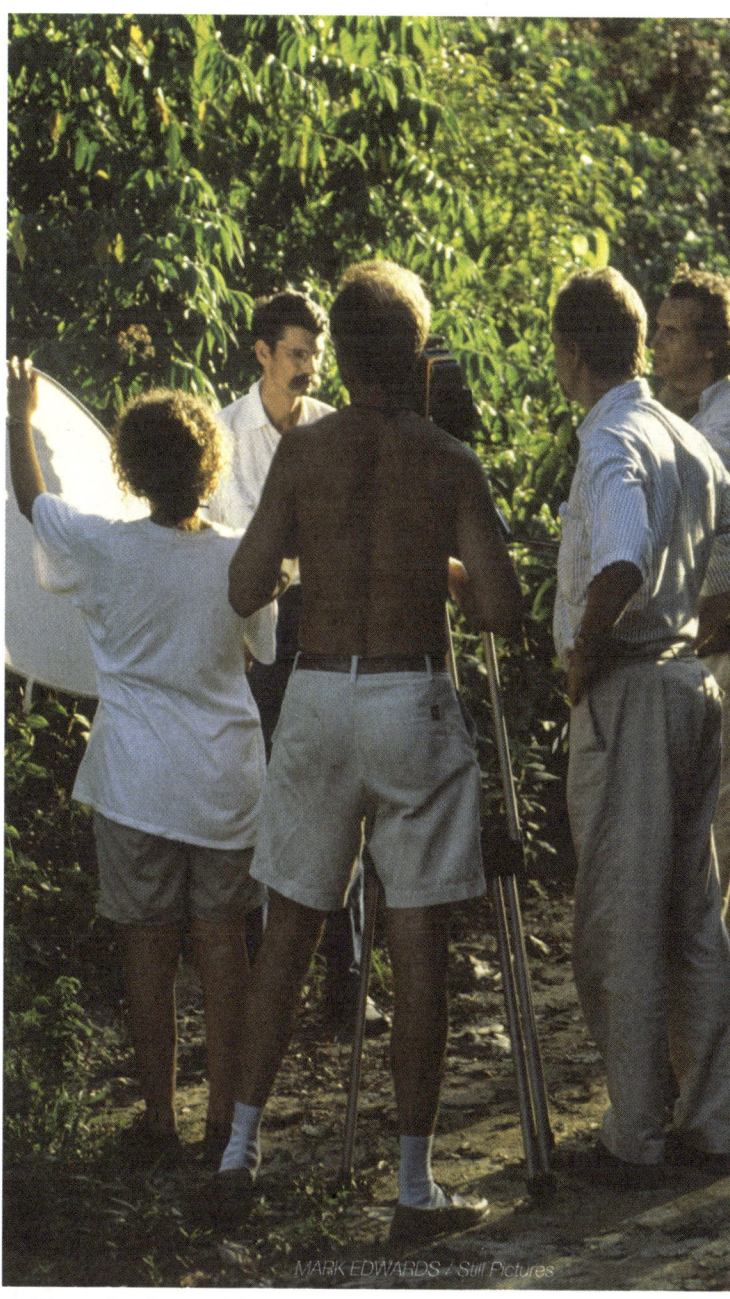

TV crew films Amazon deforestation.

VI. THE PILOT PROJECTS
Jordan, Thailand and Uganda

The first phase of HELI supported three pilot projects in Thailand, Uganda and Jordan. Country-level pilot projects aim to bring together diverse government and civil society sectors to assess and recommend integrated policies on environment and health issues as they relate to key national development priorities. The assessments test and apply the methodologies that have been developed, harnessing the combined international, regional and national resources of WHO/UNEP and the pilot project partners.

Once the assessment is complete, the initiative supports a public and technical dialogue regarding implementation of the recommendations.

- Public presentation of the assessment's recommendations and results is organized, with participation of the media.
- A workshop, hosted by the pilot project partner and including other countries in the region, is conducted to disseminate professional knowledge and build capacity for intersectoral collaboration.

Within the framework of a linked assessment of health and environment impacts, country actors choose the specific assessment tools and process best suited to local realities and needs. However, each assessment includes the following elements and procedures.

- Assessment is conducted by a core team. This team includes key experts from various sectors of government, academia and civil society.
- An advisory committee, including diverse government and civil society actors, reviews and contributes to the assessment process and its conclusions.
- When possible and appropriate, burden of disease and economic assessments are conducted in order to value the health and environment impacts of various policy options in human and monetary terms.

Summaries of each country assessment exercise and results, excerpted from the official reports of the national agencies involved, are noted in this chapter. Responsibility for the methods, accuracy of findings and recommendations as reported in the country summaries are solely the responsibility of the country teams and country institutions that administered the projects, and not WHO or UNEP.

HEALTH & ENVIRONMENT

Duncan Willets/Camerapix

1. Jordan: water is life

The issue

Jordan has one of the lowest levels of water resource availability, per capita, in the world. Water scarcity will become an even greater problem over the next two decades as the population doubles and climate change potentially makes precipitation more uncertain and variable, particularly in this region. Management of water resources is therefore a key issue facing national government authorities. Increasing overall water extraction to meet demand carries a high cost; Jordan is now accessing non-renewable water resources from fossilized deep-water aquifers.

Water quantity and quality have closley inter related health, environmental and economic dimensions which are, however, rarely linked in analysis. In terms of health, better access to safe drinking water, and higher levels of water service, are generally linked to reduced incidence of many kinds of water-borne diseases. Improving water management through reduction of domestic leakage can potentially make more water available for consumption at household level. In terms of the environment, enormous efficiencies can be achieved in water consumption not only by reducing domestic water leakage but also through use of drip irrigation technologies in agriculture – a very heavy consumer of water in most countries, including Jordan. These efficiencies not only preserve water resources in ecosystems for future use but also generate economic savings, and conserve energy used in water extraction. Building upon this basic set of associations and the best available local evidence, the Jordanian study examined the potential health, environment and economic costs/benefits of alternative water management and efficiency strategies, in order to generate a concrete set of recommendations on optimal use of a scarce resource.

Sources of water use in Jordan

SOURCE	USES IN MCM				Total Uses
	Municipal	Industrial	Irrigation	Livestock	
1. Surface water	53.3	2.5	209.7	6	271.5
- Jordan rift valley	38.5	2.5	121.2	0	162.2
- Springs	14.9	0	38	0	52.8
- Base & flood	0	0	50.5	6	56.5
2. Groundwater	185.7	34.2	252.3	1.4	473.6
- renewable	176.4	29.6	204.6	1.4	412
- nonrenewable	9.4	4.6	47.6	0	61.6
3. Treated wastewater	0	0	72	0	72
- registered	0	0	66.9	0	66.9
- not registered	0	0	5.1	0	5.1
Total	239	36.7	534	7.4	817.2

Source: Jordan Ministry of Water and Irrigation website, 2005

The process

An interdisciplinary and cross-sectoral research group, facilitated by the WHO Regional Centre for Environmental Health Activities (CEHA) in Amman, prepared a strategic environmental assessment of existing and planned water efficiency strategies. A project team consisting of members from the Ministry of Health, Ministry of Water and Irrigation, Ministry of Environment, The University of Jordan and the Jordan University of Science and Technology was selected under the guidance of an advisory committee, involving government, academic institutes and civil society.

A TOOLKIT FOR DECISION-MAKERS

The project team formed four subgroups in order to carry out the respective assessments – health, environment, water and economic valuation. Most fundamentally, the assessment considered linked environment and health impacts of alternative policy options, and the economic valuation of those impacts.

At the conclusion of the assessment process, recommendations were presented to policy-makers and a stakeholder advisory group.

They were also presented in March, 2005 at a WHO/UNEP cosponsored regional workshop, hosted by Jordan, and involving 39 professionals from 12 countries in the eastern Mediterranean region. The workshop was co-sponsored by the Children's Environment and Health Indicators Initiative. The integrated approach developed in the Jordanian pilot project is now being applied in two new Jordanian projects – the phase-out of unleaded fuel and health adaptation to climate change – and is being considered in other countries within the region.

The assessment

Having reviewed Jordan's 1997 National Water Strategy and the evidence base, the team created an innovative conceptual model to understand how water-efficiency measures in the domestic and agricultural sectors could impact upon health and environment in the country. This model formed the basis of the study and allowed the team to conceptualize the project in three complementary parts:

1. Assessment of the total investment costs involved for two selected water efficiency options for:
   a. domestic water supplies – reducing physical losses through leakage control in the supply network;
   b. agricultural water supplies – improving on-farm irrigation efficiency for drip and surface systems.
2. Formulation of indicators to assess the potential impact of these proposed measures upon human health and the environment.
3. Application of economic valuation techniques to attach economic values to the assessed health and environmental impacts and to forecast overall returns to investment.

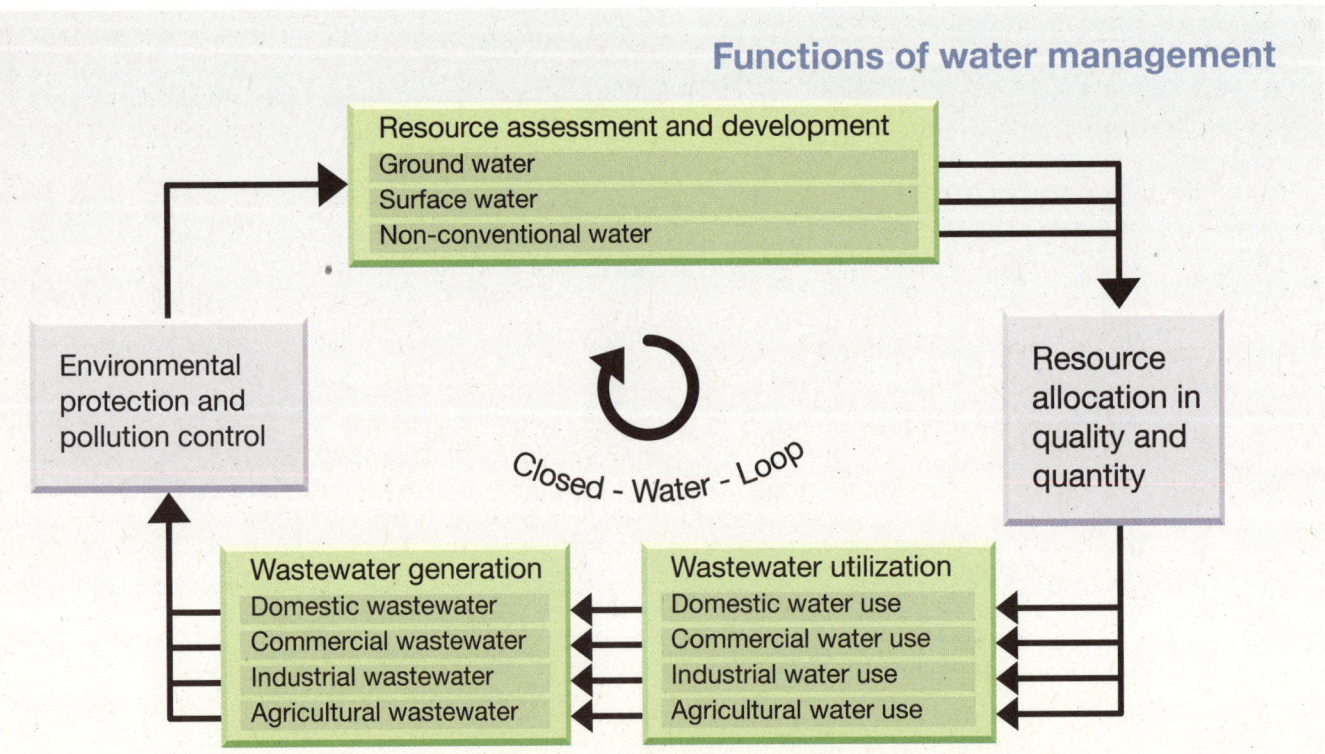

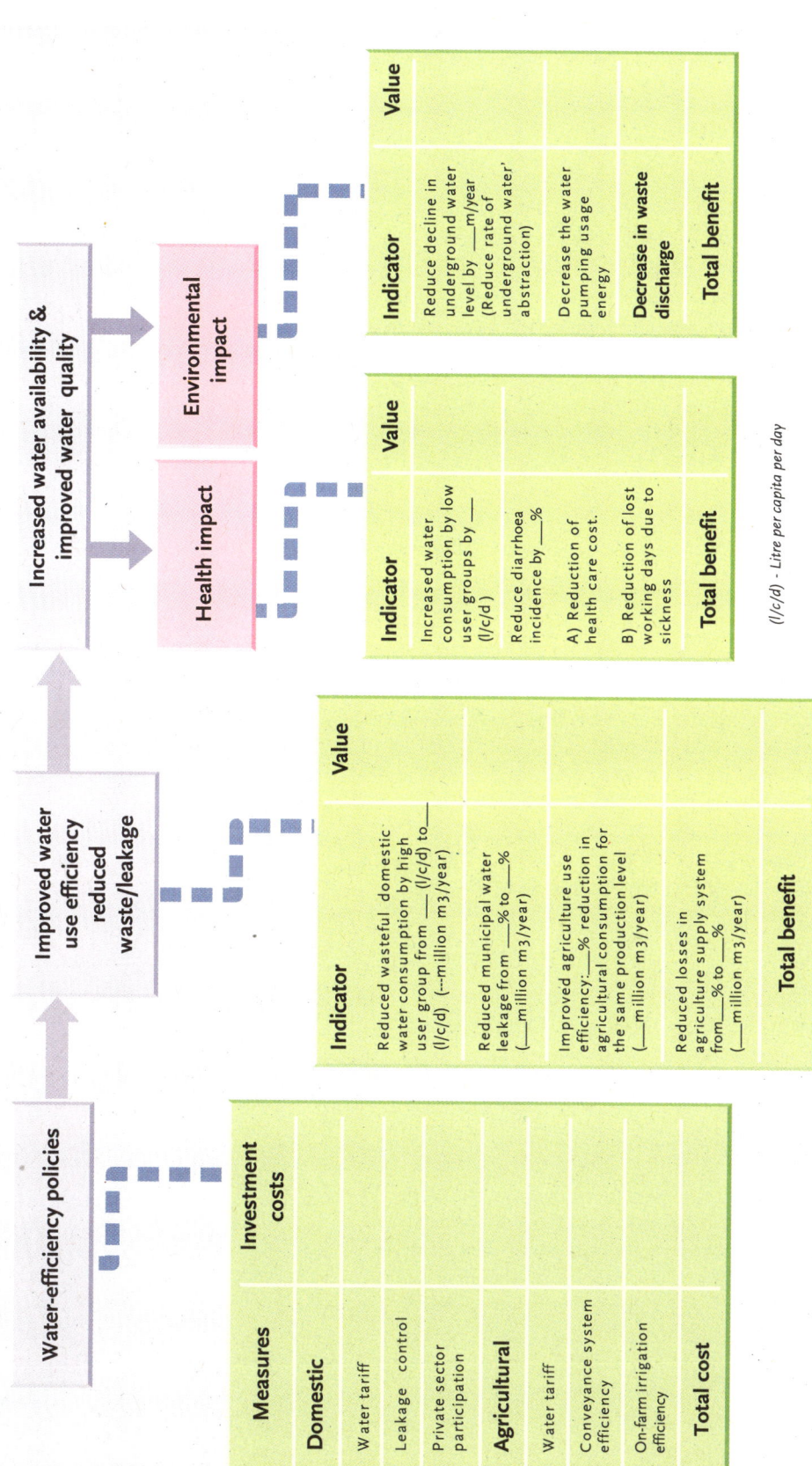

Conceptual model

(l/c/d) - Litre per capita per day

Scenarios considered in the assessment

In order to provide policy-makers with clear decision-making alternatives, the project team proposed and considered the development scenarios listed below.

1. Business-as-usual practice – maintaining current (2004) levels of investment in water-efficiency programmes.
2. Midway scenario – significant investments in the identified measures to increase water-use efficiency to levels between current and optimal. In this scenario, major capital investments in water-efficiency improvements would be made from 2005-2010; benefits considered from these investments would continue to accrue until at least 2015.
3. Mainstreaming water-use efficiency practice – major investments in water-efficiency measures to reach best achievable performance. In this scenario, major capital investments would be made 2005-2015; benefits considered from this initial capital investment would continue to accrue until at least 2025.

Key challenges faced during the assessment included: limited literature on the study topic, especially in the region and the rest of the developing world; insufficient data on health and limited secondary data on the research topic; limited time and resources for the project; and the need for improved research skills.

Health assessment component

Over 98% of the Jordanian population has access to infrastructure for a safe drinking-water supply (e.g. piped water to household; or a protected communal pump or well). However, the amount of water available for per capita consumption in these systems may vary greatly. This is related to the general water scarcity in the region, exacerbated by local and seasonal variations in the level of water available from natural sources. But domestic water consumption may also be influenced by other factors affecting level of service, such as inefficiencies in management and distribution, including inefficient use of water in agriculture; leakage in the domestic piped supply system (averaging 30%); and pricing mechanisms. In locales and in seasons where supplies available for domestic consumption are particularly limited (e.g. due to low water pressure in the piped system or low water tables in wells) households may rely upon alternative sources, including purchases from water vendors, and/or use of rainwater or other supplies stored in cisterns.

Various studies have demonstrated and measured the link between the level of water and sanitation service available to householders, levels of water consumption and diseases such as diarrhoea (Esrey, et al. 1985; Esrey, et al. 1991; Esrey 1996). Other reviews, meanwhile, have shown that investments in providing basic water and sanitation services are highly cost-beneficial in terms of time savings and other economic factors (Prüss, et al. 2002).The level of water service necessary to reduce health concerns from high to low has also been elaborated, as per the following table. In situations where access to water limits consumption to less than 50 litres per capita per day, health concerns have been defined as 'high'(Howard and Bartram 2003).

Summary of requirement for water service level to promote health

Service Level	Access measure	Needs met	Level of health concern
No access (quantity collected often below 5 l/c/d)	More than 1000m or 30 minutes total collection time	Consumption - cannot be assured Hygiene - not possible (unless practised at source)	Very high
Basic access (average quantity unlikely to exceed 20 l/c/d)	Between 100 and 1000m or 5 to 30 minutes total collection time	Consumption - should be assured Hygiene - hand washing and basic food hygiene possible; laundry/bathing difficult to assure unless carried out at source	High
Intermediate access (average quantity about 50 l/c/d)	Water delivered through one tap on-plot (or within 100m or 5 minutes total collection time)	Consumption - assured Hygiene - all basic personal and food hygiene assured; laundry and bathing should also be assured	Low
Optimal access (average quantity 100 l/c/d and above)	Water supplied through multiple taps continuously	Consumption - all needs met Hygiene - all needs should be met	Very low

The health group of the Jordan project launched a study to explore the quantitative relationship between relative levels of water consumption and diarrhoea-incidence, alongside the broader examination of environmental and economic data. A study area with representative water consumption strata was defined, including the Greater Amman area (296 000 water connections) and 16 villages in the north of Jordan.

Actual water consumption data from water bills was collected according to billing districts; diarrhoea-incidence was determined by means of data from corresponding health centre catchment areas and through calibration with the 2002 Demographic and Health Survey (DHS).

The distribution of water consumption in the study area reflected the perceived gap between the highest- and lowest-consuming groups in Jordan overall. About 20% of Jordanian consumers in the study area were found to use more than 118 litres/per capita/per day (lcd).

However, nearly 40% of consumers in the study area were found to be using less than 53 litres/per capita/per day of water, on average – a level at which health concerns may be defined as high.

Distribution of water consumption in the study area

Water consumption l/c/d	Percentage of consumers
Above 170	8%
118 -170	12%
75 -117	24%
54 - 74	17%
53 and below	39%
	100%

The comparison of local Jordanian data on average per capita water use and the burden of diarrhoeal disease indicates a correlation between higher disease incidence and lower per capita water usage. A simple linear regression of diarrhoea incidence on water consumption shows a statistically significant relationship, with diarrhoea rates higher in households that consume less water.

The results are consistent with previous studies that show that diarrhoea rates are higher among households with more difficulties accessing water, and suggest that increasing water consumption should lead to health benefits. It should be noted,

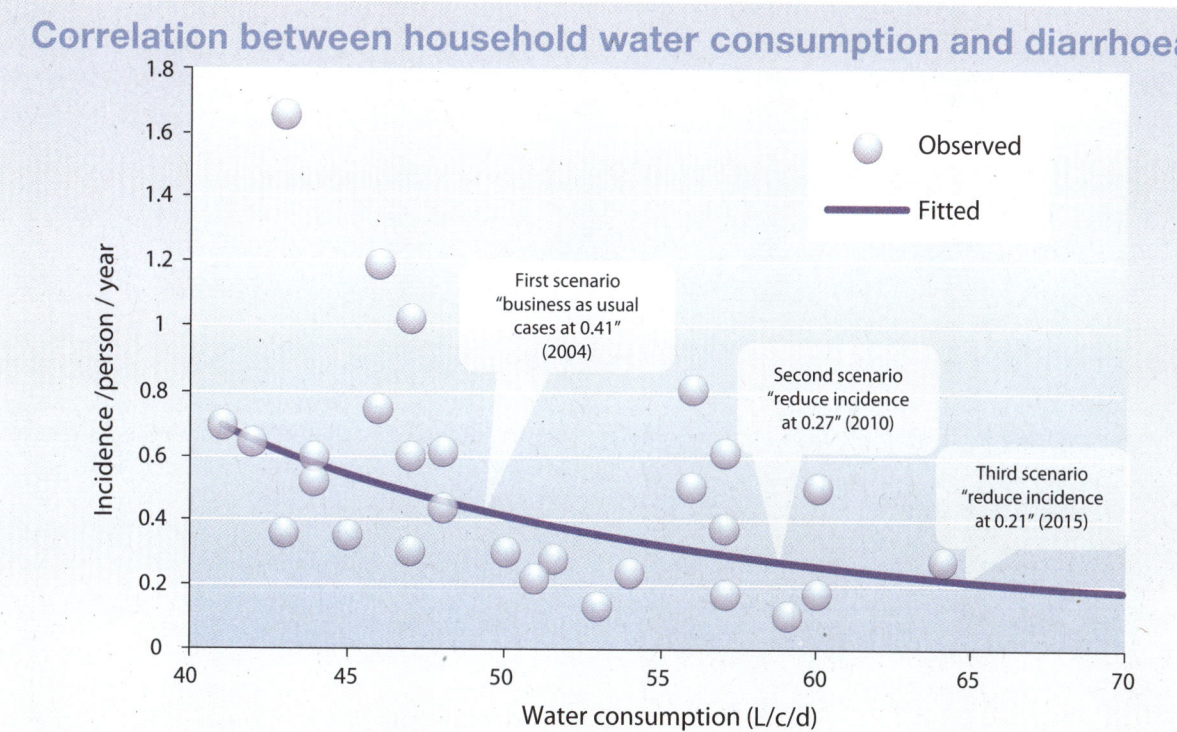

however, that the analysis was not able to take account of other potential confounding factors affecting domestic consumption (e.g. education, hygiene awareness and nutrition levels) and which could also lead to increased diarrhoea. The study also did not examine the price of water, as such, in relation to consumption. Still, while other potential confounders need to be examined in future research and analysis, the correlation provides a preliminary indication of how increased water consumption may reduce diarrhoeal disease incidence.

Water pipeline springs a leak in Jordan's Badia region.

Environmental assessment component

Reduced water usage can benefit the environment in multiple ways: more water is left in rivers and underground aquifers – enhancing ecosystems, environment and recreation; lower energy consumption for water extraction generates a secondary benefit of reduced energy production; reduced wastewater flow means less effluent disposal.

Various methodologies have been applied to provide quantitative estimates of the consequences of environmental degradation. In this assessment, two indicators were chosen that reflect environmental gains realized from better management of two critical resources – water and energy. The estimated environmental benefits of the proposed water-efficiency measures are the slowing of underground water extraction and the corresponding reduction of energy usage.

In the water sector, agriculture is by far the largest water consumer. Estimates of the water savings that could be obtained by converting all surface irrigation to drip systems and other agricultural water-efficiency measures were based upon available data on water requirements for drip irrigation compared to surface irrigation systems. There were similar estimates of the water savings that could be obtained from improved water efficiencies in the domestic water system, particularly repairs of leaks. Finally, estimates were made of the energy savings that could be obtained from reduced water extraction and pumping.

Economic valuation component

Using the data from the health and environment teams, the economics team translated the indicated investment costs and benefits into economic values. An "opportunity cost" for saved agricultural water (the value of water in its next best alternative use) was defined at the World Bank-estimated rate of Jordanian dinar (JOD) 0.44/cubic metre. Estimates of energy savings were made based on an energy cost at 2005 electricity prices – JOD 0.04/per cubic metre of water extraction. The cumulative investment costs and predicted benefits for each scenario time frame were calculated, and discounted to net present values (NPV). A discount rate of 10% per annum was used to calculate the

NPV of both investments and savings. While high by international standards, this is the rate commonly applied in Jordan due to local financial conditions. Using a lower discount rate would only increase, in fact, the estimated benefit flow.

In terms of health, it was assumed that all gains from domestic water supply efficiency measures would be redirected to those domestic users who represent the 80% of consumers in lower consumption categories. The anticipated cubic litres daily gains in water usage were used to extrapolate associated reductions in the incidence of diarrhoea/person/year for each development scenario. These were used to calculate the potential savings in mortality, morbidity and disability that could be achieved in each of the three development scenarios – represented in DALYs, associated health-care savings and lost work-days. These values were added to the predicted savings associated with the identified environmental benefits to forecast the total savings for Jordan and calculate the respective returns to investment.

Findings, conclusions and recommendations

Scenario 2, whereby leakage from the domestic water supply system was reduced from 30% to 25% between 2005 and 2010, would make available an additional 10 liters of water consumption daily (lcd) per capita without extracting additional water resources from natural environments. Efficiencies achieved in the domestic supply would be redirected to lower water consumers. Through extrapolation from the incidence of diarrhoea versus water consumption curve, it was estimated that an increase of 10 lcd corresponds to a 34% decrease in episodes of diarrhoea from 0.41 to 0.27 episodes per person per year. In addition, the investment in agricultural water efficiencies would save another 1230 million cubic metres of water over the 10-year period considered. Energy savings under Scenario 2 would be approximately 35 million Jordanian dinars (US$ 50 million) due to a lower cost of water extraction.

Scenario 3 (the maximum investment) could potentially yield a much greater water savings over the life of the investment. This could potentially provide 15 additional liters of water per capita daily to domestic consumers, through redirection of domestic water savings to lower water consumption groups, lowering diarrhoeal incidence by 49% to 0.21 episodes per person per year. In addition, increased efficiencies in agricultural water use in this scenario, largely through conversion of surface irrigation to drip systems, would result in even more significant benefits to the environment in terms of savings in agricultural water use – 3 280 million cubic meters over 20 years and energy consumption for water extraction – 64.8 million Jordanian Dinars (US$ 91.5 million).

Once the discounted economic values at a 10% discount factor are attached to the projected environmental and health benefits, the policy implications of this study become more explicit.

- Investing 178.9 million Jordanian Dinars, as per Scenario 2, would yield a benefit-cost ratio of 1.82:1
- Investing 264.7 million Jordanian Dinars as per Scenario 3, could yield a benefit-cost ratio of 2.39:1

Overall benefit-cost analysis of water efficiency measures

Scenarios	Environment/ water resource benefits[1] MJD	Health benefits[2] MJD	Environment/ energy resource benefits[3] MJD	Investment costs MJD	Benefit / cost ratio
I	0	0	0	0	–
II. Capital investment (2005-2010) Benefit stream (2005-2015)	262.70	27.30	34.98	178.87	1.82
III. Capital investment (2005-2015) Benefit stream (2005-2025)	463.10	60.95	64.79	246.67	2.39

All values are represented in Net Present Value, using a discount rate of 10% per annum. Million Jordanian Dinars (MJD)

Footnotes
1. Environment/water resource benefits: This represents the economic value of net water savings obtained from improved efficiencies in each scenario, and derived largely from savings in the agriculture sector, since domestic water savings would be redirected towards the lowest water consumers, for health benefits.
2. Health benefits: This represents the economic value both of the DALYs gained (avoided morbidity and mortality), and savings in direct cost of treatment/care of water-borne diseases in the scenarios.
3. Environment/energy resource benefits: This represents the economic value of net savings in energy power consumption for purposes of water pumping.

The CBA ratios confirm the cost-beneficial nature of investments in water-efficiency measures, due to the health, environment and economic benefits that can be enjoyed. Many other benefits to quality of life and well-being – including some which are difficult to quantify – also could be realized as a result of improved water efficiency.

Based upon the study results, the assessment recommended an acceleration of planned government investments in water efficiency in order to realize more rapidly the projected numerous benefits between health, environment and economic benefits. In addition, economic measures should be taken to support water usage adequate for health among lower consumption groups, and discourage excessive and wasteful consumption of water among the more intensive water consumers.

These interventions could take the form of health-sensitive water tariff structures, other regulatory and economic instruments, public awareness tools and the use of water-saving devices. The cost-benefit (benefit-cost) ratios also suggest that the efficiency measures could be self-sustaining through ongoing reinvestment of the accrued savings from the selected water-efficiency measures. The substantial health and environmental savings predicted by the study support the overall aim of the Jordan Water Strategy – achieving "the highest possible efficiency in the conveyance, distribution, application and use" of water resources.

For more information and full report:

Health and Environment Linkages Initiative (HELI) - Jordan Pilot, WHO/CEHA, Amman, 2006.

www.who.int/heli/pilots/en/

2. Thailand: reducing environmental risks and enhancing health through sustainable agriculture

The issue

Thai agricultural policy has been blamed often for promoting the use of pesticides without adequate, effective control mechanisms. Inappropriate and excessive pesticide use can have long-term impacts on health and environment, as well as impeding the export of Thai products. Periodically this issue has been a focus of economic and political concern.

According to Thai Department of Agriculture (DOA) records, the use of pesticides has increased dramatically over the past 20 years. In 2003, the quantity of active ingredient imported into Thailand was 79 837 476 kg, more than twice the amount recorded in 1996. Organophosphates comprised the largest proportion of the imported volume – 55%. The pesticide industry is currently worth 9116 million Baht (US$ 225 million) per year (IPM Danida 2003). Between 3000 and 4500 people are reported to suffer from acute pesticide poisoning in the occupational setting every year, although this is considered conservative, as there is severe under-reporting. While there are no routine surveys of environmental contamination at national level, environmental sampling has indicated the widespread presence of soil and water residues of certain organochlorine chemicals, including endosulfan and DDT. DDT is a persistent organic pollutant whose use was severely restricted by the Stockholm convention of May 2004 (WHO 2004b); endosulfan is banned or has strictly-limited use in a wide range of countries, including Thailand.

There are not only public health concerns but also economic dimensions to the pesticide issue. A report by the Department of Agriculture's Office of Agricultural Economics (OAE) estimates that the economic cost of returned agricultural products has risen consistently from 284 million Baht (US$ 11 million) in 1992 to 1216 million Baht (US$ 27.8 million) in 2001.

The demand to support more sustainable agricultural practices that contribute to health, the environment and economic development, thus has resonance throughout wide sectors of Thai society. But supporting safer pesticide use alongside viable alternatives (e.g. integrated pest management) is no easy task. At present, policies controlling agricultural pesticides are set forth in the Hazardous Substance Act (B.E. 2535), under the responsibility of the Hazardous Substance Committee, composed of appointed government officers and technocrats. Public involvement in the policy process as well as in the monitoring and evaluation systems is largely absent. Furthermore, research data on toxicity of agricultural pesticides submitted for the registration of toxic substances are limited to the manufacturers' own laboratory studies, usually performed outside of the country in conditions that may differ greatly from the local Thai context. It is important, then, that the knowledge regarding the full range of health, environment, social and economic costs and benefits of alternative policies be explored and synthesized in order to support effective decisions. In line with this goal, an environment and health impact assessment of agricultural pesticide use was carried out by the Thai country project of HELI, in order to support sound policy decisions at farmer level.

Overall, the relationship between pesticide use, environment and health impacts can be represented in the conceptual framework of the

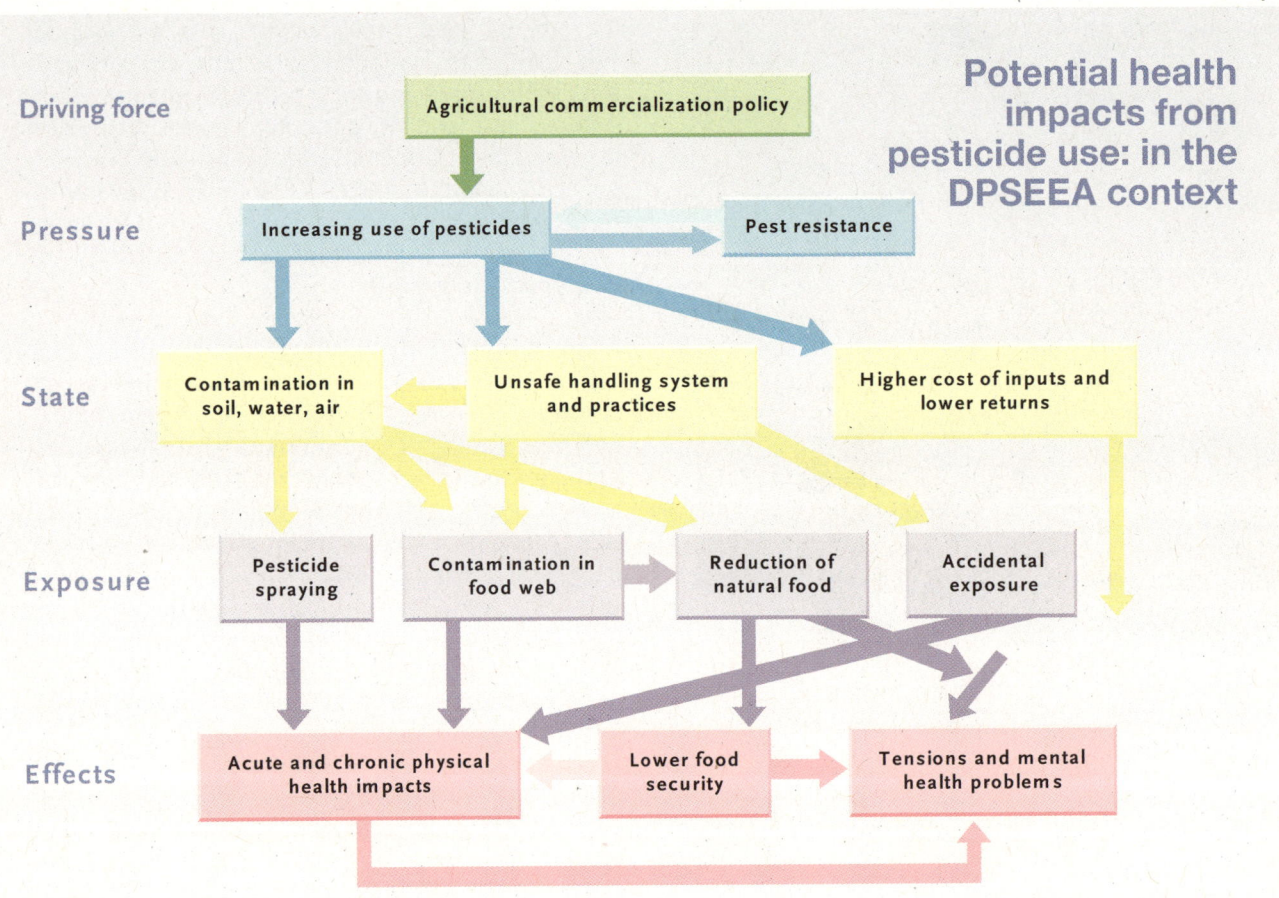

Potential health impacts from pesticide use: in the DPSEEA context

DPSEEA model (driving forces, pressures, state, exposure, effects, actions) developed at WHO to describe the more general causal relationship between political, social and economic drivers, and environment and health impacts (Corvalán, et al. 2000). Actions to address these impacts were the focus of this HELI country project.

The process

An environment and health impact assessment (EHIA) of the use of agrochemicals was conducted. This was coordinated by the Thai Department of Health and the Health Systems Research Institute, in collaboration with the Thai Food and Drug Administration, Departments of Agriculture and Agricultural Extension, Office of Natural Resources and Environmental Policy and Planning and a range of civil society NGOs. The goal was to provide an evidence-based assessment of agricultural pesticides for sustainable agricultural development, from a health and environment perspective.

The process included national review and analysis of existing policies and legislation and the development of new national policy recommendations.

Subsequently, a local-level deliberative policy assessment of policies in the Tung Tong sub-district provided a valuable model for a participatory public policy process and also filled important data gaps about local health and the environmental impacts of pesticides. This was a key feature of the Thai project. It is unique in that it captured conventional forms of data and evidence along with a dialogue between diverse stakeholders. The assessment also supported Thailand's own drive to institutionalize health impact assessment (HIA) as part of its sustainable healthy public policy. Findings were presented in June 2006 at a workshop attended by over 40 participants representing the health, environment, and agriculture sectors from 15 South-East Asia and Western Pacific countries. Participants recognized the sustainable management of agrochemicals as a major issue throughout the region, and endorsed the need to address the issue using a knowledge management approach that takes into account health, environment, and economic considerations, as an integrated contribution to sustainable development. The meeting recommended that the project approach should be integrated into regional initiatives, such as the Ministerial Regional Forum on Environment and Health for South-East and East Asian Countries, and implementation projects of the new global Strategic Approach to International Chemicals Management (SAICM).

Even prior to the workshop, however, the results of the Tung Tong assessment were being acted upon at the grass roots. New, far-reaching targets and goals aimed at reducing excessive pesticide use and building capacity for healthy farming methods integrating environmental management tools into pest-control strategies, were being incorporated into the local development plan.

The shared vision in the Tung Tong community development master plan stated that: "Tung Tong will be free from the use of toxic agricultural pesticides in the next 10 years, through the promotion of organic agriculture, accompanied by the promotion of local wisdom and culture, and strengthening of local communities." (See local policy actions and recommendations).

The assessment method

The assessment process in Thailand comprised seven main steps, as illustrated in the model. These were (i) a deliberative policy analysis, e.g. a national dialogue involving all relevant government organizations and stakeholders in a series of one-day policy workshops, which provided a more complete understanding of how knowledge is used in public process regarding pesticide uses and agricultural policy; and (ii) a literature review to survey and compile evidence about the environmental, health and economic impacts of pesticide use and alternative agriculture in the Thai context.

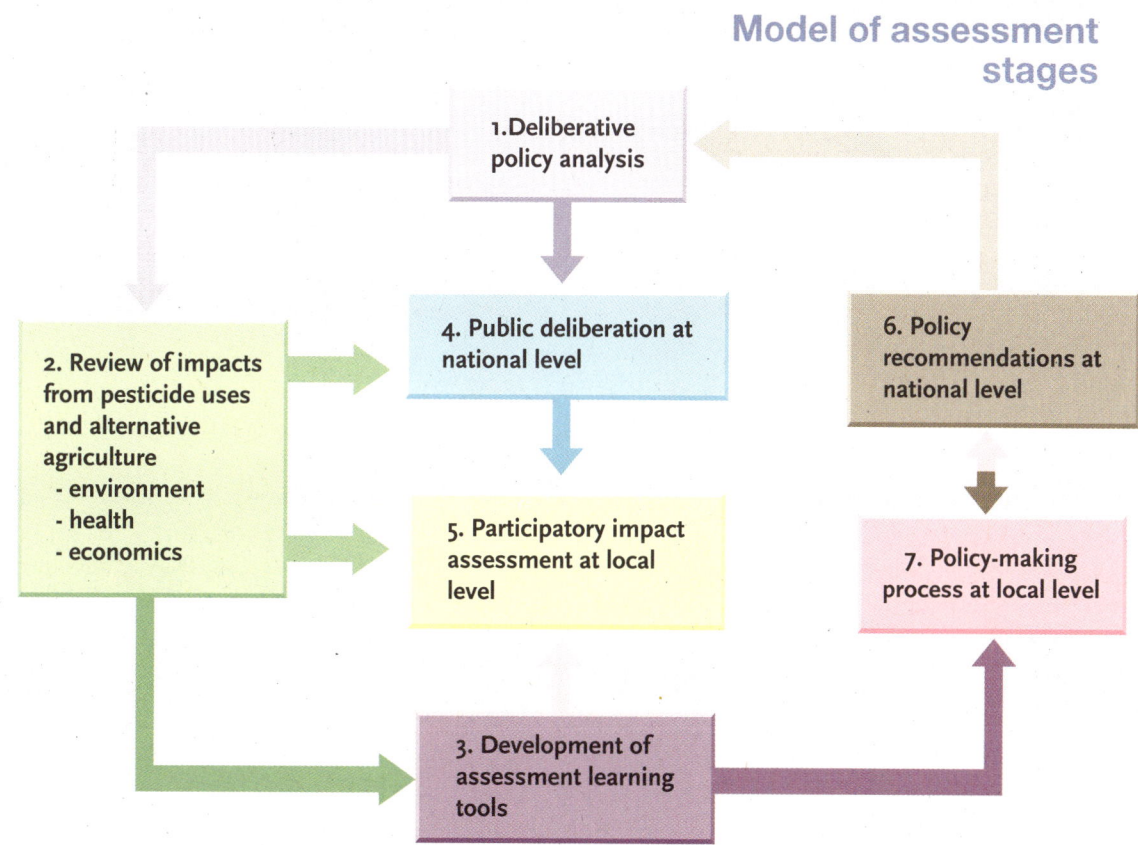

Model of assessment stages

The results of the first two steps were fed into the development of (iii) an impact assessment learning tool; and (iv) a public deliberation process at national level (through a policy workshop). These steps contributed to (v) a local level participatory impact assessment which was the core of the HELI case study. This filled major data gaps about the health impacts of pesticides and synthesized knowledge about health, environment and economic impacts, including local knowledge and views by diverse stakeholder groups. Outcomes from all of these steps contributed, finally, to (vi) policy recommendations at national level; and (vii) a participatory policy-making process at local level. In the future, results of the latter two can be used again as relevant direct experiences for the deliberative policy analysis.

Initial findings

National deliberative policy analysis

The national dialogue with stakeholders, involving three one-day workshops in Bangkok, concluded that excessive pesticide use is a significant problem throughout Thailand. In addition, stakeholders emphasized that policies encouraging safe or reduced pesticide use must be integrated with support for the development of alternative pest control methods or methods of agricultural practice.

At the same time, the workshops revealed that gaps in integrated data and knowledge collection and knowledge management regarding safe pesticide use, alternative methods, health, environment and economic impacts are critical obstacles to improved policies. Most decision-makers frame their knowledge and data needs in a single dimension confined to their own areas of responsibility regarding pesticides.

Analysis of the key governmental and non-governmental stakeholders involved in pesticide policy also revealed diversity in the values, beliefs and perceptions regarding pesticide risks, impacts and policies. Still, like-minded civil society actors have banded together to support policy directions, as in The Advocacy Coalition Network. This is an umbrella for four initiatives: Sustainable Agriculture Promotion, Decreasing

Market in southern Thailand.

Pesticide Use Promotion, Safe Food Promotion and Pesticide Use Promotion. Between these four, gaps in knowledge can lead to conflicts of interest and even social polarization. Greater knowledge-sharing can reinforce collaboration, increasing the coherence of policy positions and strategies regarding regulatory loopholes, alternative policy developments, integrated planning tools and participatory surveillance systems.

The health dimension

According to the Bureau of Epidemiology, Ministry of Public Health, from 1990 to 1999 between 2599 and 4827 people annually were reported to have suffered from acute pesticide poisoning due to occupational exposures. Some 80% of these cases involved farmers. In blood tests performed by the Department of Health to screen for exposure to organophosphate and carbamate pesticides, the proportion of agricultural workers determined to be at risk of health damage increased from 17% to 24% between 1992 and 2001.

It must be emphasized that these statistics tend to under-represent the true dimensions of the problem, since most farmers suffering from pesticide poisoning are treated at home – it has been reported that only 21% see a doctor. Of other workers suffering from pesticide poisoning only 2.4% go to hospital (Muksuwan 2005). Tests and surveillance by the Ministry of Public Health and other agencies have indicated that about one third of the fresh products placed on the local Thai market may contain pesticide residues above permissible limits (Poapongsakorn, et al.1998; IPM Danida 2003).

Records of the chronic effects of pesticides are found rarely in Thailand due to the limited amount of research and surveillance on the relationship between long-term pesticide exposure and subsequent illness. However, there is increasing evidence about the possible links between long-term exposure to pesticides and an increase in the risk of developmental and reproductive disorders, immune-system disruption, endocrine disruption, impaired nervous-system function and the development of certain cancers.

The environmental dimension

In Thailand, pesticide contamination is monitored primarily by researchers from the relevant public agencies, including the Pollution Control Department (PCD), Ministry of Natural Resources and Environment, Department of Agriculture (DOA) and the Ministry of Agriculture and Cooperatives.

A key finding of the literature review was that incidents of environmental pesticide contamination are reported generally case-by-case, not monitored routinely on a nationwide basis. The Department of Environmental Quality Promotion does not recognize pesticides as a major source of water and soil pollution despite research evidence indicating that soils and surface waters may be contaminated by certain kinds of organochlorine pesticides. In particular, DDT, carbofuran, dicofol, endosulfan, mevinphos and paraquat have been found often at above-standard levels in both surface water and soils. In one such study, PCD detected contamination levels of DDT at 68% and carbofuran at 46% in soil samples. In another study, endosulfan contamination was found in 76% of surface-water samples collected (Research Institute for Health Sciences 2004).

However, most reported data on pesticide contamination indicate levels below the relevant standards, providing little incentive to study their impacts on physical and biological resources. The DOA and Integrated Pest Management (IPM) groups have made many attempts to study the impact of pesticide use on biodiversity on farms. The comparative study on biodiversity between farm fields using the IPM technique and those using pesticides has shown that the number of natural predators in an IPM field is significantly higher than those in farms using agricultural chemicals. The average number of species of predators in fields increased from 1.58 to 2.58 after farmers ran their farms under IPM techniques (Research Center of Applied Economics 2001).

The economic dimension

The annual quantity and value of imported pesticides is well-documented, but it is difficult to analyse the economic impacts of pesticides at the local scale as there is no record of pesticide distribution or use by region. Nonetheless, numerous targeted studies have been conducted on the economic impacts of pesticide use by agencies such as the Office of Agricultural Economics (OAE) and the DOA, in conjunction with the DOA agricultural school programme. The latter also has provided basic instruction in sustainable agricultural methods (e.g. IPM) and operational cost accounting. An OAE report found that pesticides and fertilizers account for around 30% of total farm costs, or 6000 Baht (US$154) annually (Research Institute for Health Sciences 2004). This suggests that farmers could reduce their costs by stopping or reducing the use of these chemicals.

Drawing upon before and after cost comparisons by farmers enrolled in the agricultural school programme, DOA concluded that pesticide costs could be reduced by more than one quarter, from approximately 41 Baht (US$ 1.08) to 28 Baht (US$ 0.74) per rai (1 rai = 1600 square metres and 0.4 acres) of land if farmers implemented IPM techniques. IPM supports the optimal use of beneficial insects, natural predators and other biological controls to curb populations of harmful insects, bacteria and fungus, alongside judicious use of modern chemicals. For farmers who completed the programme, costs were reduced and their total incomes increased slightly (Research Center of Applied Economics 2001).

In reality, the benefit of reducing or eliminating the use of pesticides is even greater as these figures do not take account of health and environment benefits. These have no monetary value within the current economic system; even farmers' economic losses associated with the return of tainted agricultural products typically is not quantified. Researchers have estimated that the external costs of chemical pesticide use in terms of health impacts, pesticide management, regulation, quality control and research into pesticides, may be as high as 5481 million Baht (US$ 144.52 million), roughly equivalent to the annual value of pesticides sold on the local Thai market (Jungbluth 1996; Mörner 2002).

The greatest gap identified by the literature review is the lack of integrated management of knowledge related to the health, environment and economic impacts of pesticide use. Most recorded data are in a format specific to their own use and fail to meet the requirements of other studies. For example, it is difficult to perform an effective health risk assessment – critical in any epidemiological study – if there are no data on the distribution of a particular pesticide. Without systematic data linkages to support health risk assessment, studies are handicapped from the start. Two other problems with the absence of integrated knowledge management are given below.

- Under-reporting of pesticide-related illness by farmers who lack awareness about the links between health and pesticide exposures; in turn this limits the relevance of broader health impact assessments of pesticide exposure.

- The dearth of systematic and comprehensive health impact assessments, in turn, hinders development of more effective policy control mechanisms.

Alternative agriculture in Thailand

Although official policies that effectively support safe and judicious pesticide use have been slow to develop, civil society organizations have been active in promoting changed practices from the bottom up. Alternative agricultural movements have been an important vehicle for building capacity in environmental management strategies. Some of the most common methods in Thailand include: agroforestry, integrated farming, new theory agriculture, organic farming, natural farming and IPM. In general and to varying degrees, such practices aim to enhance yields and control pests through better management/manipulation of the agroecosystem rather than through chemical applications alone. Tactics include traditional tools such as crop rotation, soil conservation practices, use of organic fertilizers and pesticides, and control of pests by encouraging natural predators. Such methods may generate certain economic benefits, alongside health and environment gains, e.g. improved food security through sustainable soil fertility. However, beyond the narrow cost-benefit analysis of inputs and outputs to a single crop, such economic costs and benefits typically are not well-defined.

Harvesting organic and fair trade jasmine rice in Thailand with a farmer association.

Certain studies have sought to attribute economic value to alternative agricultural techniques. The Center for Applied Economics Research at Kasetsart University provides instruction in cost-benefit analysis as part of its agricultural school programme. It found a positive statistical correlation between IPM practices and reduced pesticide costs, increased productivity and decreased health costs. These were statistically significant at 95%, 95% and 90% respectively (Research Center of Applied Economics 2001). By incorporating regulatory costs into its analysis of IPM practices, this study provides a greater policy orientation to the economic assessment, expanding its scope beyond the individual farm level. Yet although economic costs and benefits to health and the environment are valued fully, they are noted only as a statistical correlation. One key barrier to the generation of a full economic assessment is the absence of basic epidemiological and eco-environmental data on pesticide impacts on farmer health, soil fertility, natural predator populations and pest resistance – which could be converted into economic values.

Rather than relying on just one cash crop, integrated farming cultivates an ecologically harmonious mix of crops that sustains soil fertility, deters harmful pests and increases ecological resilience (e.g. to extreme weather and losses from erosion). Kasetsart University's Faculty of Economics has piloted another approach to cost-benefit valuation of these methods. Their study concluded that the early stage of integrated farming produces a lower net income than mono-agriculture, where short-term economies of scale may be realized. However, after eight to nine years, integrated farming is more cost-beneficial. In addition, the study indicated that households practicing integrated farming methods could save up to 40% of their expenses, primarily in purchases of food and agrochemicals. Overall, the study concluded that the economic returns of integrated farming were significantly higher than those of mono-culture when gains such as enhanced economic security through reduced losses from disasters, soil fertility and quality were considered. In addition, integrated faming practices also reduced annual labour costs by as much as 25 000 Baht (US$ 551) in some households. Yet although this study illustrates the positive environmentally-related costs and benefits of alternative agricultural practices, it is a major weakness that it fails to quantify the related health benefits that might accrue from reduced pesticide exposures (Research Center of Applied Economics 2001).

Deliberative assessment of health and environment impacts at local level

One of the unique features of the Thai HELI project was the deliberative impact assessment conducted at the local level. This participatory exercise aimed to generate a model of integrated knowledge synthesis, community learning and stimulation of bottom-up policy change. The impact assessment was carried out as a case study in the Tung Tong Subdistrict of Sai Thong Wattana District in Kampaeng Phet Province. Agricultural products such as rice and sugar cane are the primary source of income in this community. Pesticides, fertilizers and plant hormones have been used heavily. For example, this study found that in rice cultivation the average local farm household used 6181 litres of chemicals per year (320 litres per rai of land) for one crop; and 8302 litres per household (315 litres per rai) for two crops per year.

HELI team joins in the rice harvest effort in a Thai village taking part in the health and environment assessment of agricultural pesticide practices.

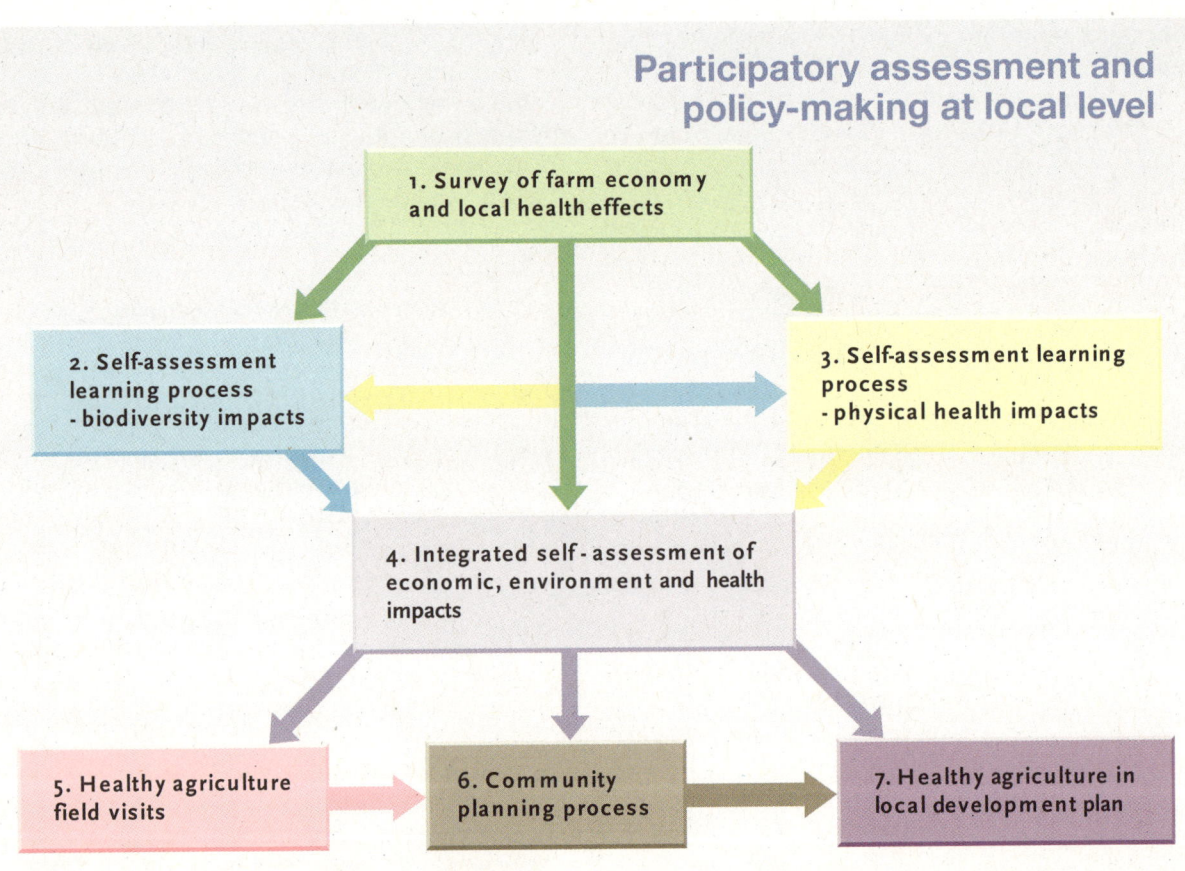

Participatory assessment and policy-making at local level

Members of the Thai HELI team on a visit to Tung Tong subdistrict.

The Tung Tong assessment involved a cross-disciplinary group of 50 community members including farmers, community leaders, local administration members, community health staff and volunteers, and local agricultural officers. The assessment process included seven steps, outlined in the figure above.

The assessment began with a learning process in which group members exchanged knowledge and experiences. A community biodiversity survey identified the impacts of chemicals on flora and fauna; a chemical pesticides utilization survey identified local trends in pesticide usage. Body mapping of illnesses helped pinpoint associations between pesticide exposures and health impacts. A field trip to another community offered the group an example of how others have addressed pesticide problems. Thus the process generated knowledge gains within the group and new data on health and environment linkages and risks associated with local chemical pesticide use. Key findings and linkages are described in the following box (page 66).

HEALTH ENVIRONMENT

Results of the participatory assessment in Tung Tong sub-district

- Pesticides are the main factor implicated in the deterioration of certain local food resources and biodiversity, including snake-headed fish, frog, freshwater prawn, land crab, ground lizard and grasshopper. Some chemicals affect "beneficial insects" such as bees and wasps.
- Although endosulfan has been banned in Thailand for three years, local farmers can buy it easily, indeed it is the second most popular chemical used in the area. Endosulfan is an organochlorine pesticide categorized by WHO as moderately toxic to humans (WHO 2004).
- 67.1% of farmers spray pesticides themselves: on average 41.5% spray once a month, 62.2% spray more than 5000 litres per year.
- Average pesticide and chemical fertilizer costs are around one third of total production costs in rice production and one fifth in sugar-cane production.
- 61.2% of farmers mix more than one pesticide into each spraying, leading to higher risks of exposure and toxicity.
- 46.3% of farmers mix chemical pesticides without using gloves.
- 69.1% of farmers never use eyeglasses or masks to protect their eyes.
- 34.0% of farmers engaged in pesticide applications fail to wash their hands before eating or drinking.
- 62.8% of farmers are fully soaked by pesticides during spraying.
- 35.6% of farmers always wash tools for mixing and spraying pesticides in local water sources.
- 73.1% of farmers keep their pesticides in places that children can reach easily.
- 43.0% of farmers have experienced "intermediate" health effects from pesticide spraying (e.g. blurred vision, spasmodic eyelids, choking feeling in the chest, nausea and vomiting).
- Only 35% of farmers who experienced negative effects from pesticide spraying went to the hospital or a health care provider; 65% recovered on their own.

Local policy actions and recommendations

The deliberative impact assessment in Tung Tong Sub-district yielded immediate and far-ranging results. These demonstrate the power and efficacy of such a local-level process as a lever for generating broader actions and policy changes.

The participatory collection and assessment of health and environmental risk information boosted awareness of the impacts of excessive pesticide use among farmers and the local administration, and spurred interest in healthy farming alternatives. Thus the group learning process was the launching point for a participatory public policy process whereby group members were motivated to become involved in community planning and to integrate the findings and lessons learnt into local development plans and policies.

Following the conclusion of the impact assessment, a community planning process was launched. This set up far-reaching targets and goals for the reduction of pesticide use, and support for healthy farming alternatives, to be integrated into the local development plan (see below).

New targets for the Tung Tong development plan

- 2006: reduce pesticide use by 30%.
- 2006: apply biological controls to 80% of paddy fields.
- 2009: 30% of rice and other farm products will be pesticide-free products.
- 2015: all Tung Tong sub-district will be a pesticide-free area. Increase freshwater animals by approximately 300 000 living organisms.
- Increase organic fertilizer use to more than 2 tons per village to improve soil fertility and increase crop rotation in paddy fields by 30%.
- Organize women farmer groups for healthy agriculture and income-generating activities.
- Save farmer households 5-10% annually in farm costs, through healthy agriculture alternatives.

Frans Lemmens / Still Pictures

While the proposed plan is awaiting local council approval, many of its elements already have been implemented independently by the stakeholders involved in the process. In addition, the Tung Tong local administration has already taken the following steps:

- approved a new budget supporting local farmers experimenting with biological control methods to replace pesticide uses;
- set up local groups organized around pesticide-free agriculture;
- introduced the IPM farmer field school approach, in collaboration with the agricultural extension office, to create a learning process and technical consultancy for local farmers;
- introduced a local course in primary care for pesticide-affected cases;
- local farmers are now implementing reduced pesticide practices on their own farms;
- local development plan is in process of final approval by local administrative council.

Conclusion and recommendations

Based upon the lessons learnt in the local Tung Tong sub-district case study, certain assessment tools and methods for policy implementation and surveillance were identified as particularly relevant for integrating health and environment concerns into policies on agrochemical use. Some are discussed in more detail below.

Link integrated impact assessment and IPM with improved self-assessment models, learning tools and exercises

Integrated impact assessment methods have good potential to strengthen and supplement capacity-building for IPM. Self-assessment tools and learning exercises, whereby farmers themselves document and disseminate the benefits and positive consequences of different farming practices, are extremely important. It is crucial to create community participation and empowerment mechanisms that give all stakeholders an appreciation of the linkages between health, environment and ecosystems, society and the economy. By understanding the risks, farmers will be motivated to protect their own right to live in a healthy environment. Policy-makers must also take part in the learning process so that they are aware of issues and can take appropriate actions.

Analyse authority relationships of stakeholders in policy processes

Clarification of authority relationships among all stakeholders in policy processes should be an essential element of self-assessment and group learning models and exercises. Understanding of these relationships provides entry points for public policy mobilization.

Develop an integrated community planning tool

A tool for community planning of alternative agriculture and pesticide reductions, using the lessons learnt in this HELI study, would support integration of the health, environment, economic and social aspects of agriculture into participatory planning processes for community development. Public participation should be incorporated into the early phases of development plans and proposals so as to give community views more legitimacy and standing with decision-makers.

Create a model for a local participatory surveillance system

Develop a tool to guide and facilitate surveillance of pesticide use by local farmers and local administrations. This should cover the entire plant-to-harvest cycle, including pesticide disposal and environmental restoration. Over time, the implementation of such a local tool could be built into a broader provincial and national surveillance system, filling an important gap in existing surveillance mechanisms.

Conduct hazard analysis of regulatory loopholes

This idea applies total quality management (TQM), as described in standard hazard analysis and critical control point systems (HACCP), to the pesticide regulatory system. This analysis would focus on actual nationwide pesticide control practices to explore and identify the loopholes and critical control points (such as storage and waste management) that may cause hazards or problems in the field. This will inform a national road map for filling or bridging identified gaps, improving systems and strengthening policy mechanisms of the regulatory system.

Support alternative policy development processes

A deliberative policy process framed around the values of living healthily together provides an opportunity for all policy actors to exchange perspectives and knowledge needs and to draw upon all relevant experiences to understand the multifactorial health and environmental impacts of pesticides. This deliberative process, supplemented by conventional research, is likely to propose healthier solutions than more conventional methods of data collection and evidence development alone. Dialogue involving groups with different values opens the minds of both experts and generalists to alternative ideas and practices. As seen in the Tung Tong case, such deliberative policy processes also can yield a complete and integrated understanding of the necessary and feasible investments and actions required from various social and economic actors to achieve change.

Implementation and follow-up of public policy recommendations

Many policy recommendations can be implemented prior to formal approval – through voluntary mechanisms (e.g. farmers using IPM methods). Conversely, formal policy approval by the local administrator does not guarantee implementation. Farmers and stakeholders therefore need to be involved in following-up, monitoring and evaluating plans. Developing policy networks inside and beyond the community can help to reinforce and strengthen policy implementation.

Recommended policy actions: national and local levels

The broader HELI review also yielded an integrated set of recommendations for policy actions, summarized in the table below. These are ordered in the hierarchy of the DPSEEA framework described in Section I, highlighting the entry points for integrated actions that address the broader political and economic drivers as well as the individual health exposures/impacts that are the final consequence of excessive pesticide use.

Thai women harvest tea leaves

Recommended actions for protecting health and environment from increasing pesticide use in Thailand

Levels of action	National level
1. Driving force	o Unify agricultural policy based on sustainable development principles that promote health and environment together with commercial competition.
2. Pressure	o Set clear goals and policy measures for reducing the use of chemical agricultural pesticides throughout the country (e.g. 50% reduction over 5 years). o Set goals and supporting means for all possible healthy agricultural practices. o Articulate clearly the national commercial advantages and "niche market" opportunities of very high quality assurance and agricultural products free of residual pesticides.
3. State	o Place more stringent controls on the import, distribution and advertisement of chemical agricultural pesticides. o Mainstream a participatory public policy process where all stakeholders take part, equally and openly, in the policy decision process. o Mandate central and local governments and communities to cooperate in establishing integrated community-based action plans applying IPM principles and other alternative agricultural practices. o Encourage agricultural producers and exporters to support the research and development of safe agricultural production and alternative agricultural practices.
4. Exposure	o Develop reliable chemical agricultural pesticide information system that covers the whole route of pesticide use from import to farm, for local and national levels. o Urgently develop health, environment, social and EIA systems for both short- and long-term policy decision support and implementation. o Promote effective communication and education about safe use of chemical agricultural pesticides and alternative agriculture/pest-control practices. o Promote a learning process involving stakeholders on health, environment and other impacts o agricultural pesticides. o Establish reliable quality control and safety systems for agricultural products.
5. Effect	o Anchor policy in the effective use of knowledge and information derived from situation analysis and approved by all sectors. o Support safe use of agricultural pesticides with diminishing trend according to the goal established. o Decrease health and environmental risks and impacts. o Restore degraded environments and ecosystems. o Enhance Thailand's reputation for high quality agricultural products thereby generating sustained producer, consumer and trading partner reliance on Thai products. o Increase national income from agriculture.

For more information and full report see:

Rodsawad J, et al. *Environment and health impact assessment of agricultural pesticide application for policy decision support*. Bangkok, Thai Ministry of Public Health and Health Systems Research Institute, 2006.

www.who.int/heli/pilots/uganda/en/

Local level

- Articulate a healthy and environmentally-friendly agricultural policy in community development plans.

- Set goals and policy measures for reducing the use of chemical agricultural pesticides at local levels.
- Set goals and supporting measures for all possible healthy agricultural practices at local levels.
- Present a vision for all agricultural areas to become free of hazardous agricultural chemical usages in an appropriate time frame.
- Instill participatory public policy process principles into the community development planning process.

- Establish sale, marketing and advertising control mechanisms at local levels, using both legislative and social levers.
- Establish a health and environmental impact monitoring mechanism to be used by communities and local governments.
- Establish community-strengthening mechanisms in line with the leading principles and concepts of Thailand's 10th National Economic and Social Development Plan.
- Support central government organizations in working together with local administrations and communities to promote the implementation of IPM and alternative agricultural practices which reduce or eliminate unnecessary use of chemical pesticides.

- Develop reliable chemical agricultural pesticide information and monitoring system that covers the whole route of pesticide use at local level.
- Develop primary medical services and local health surveillance systems for the control and reduction of agricultural pesticide risks and health impacts.
- Promote effective communication and education about safe use of chemical agricultural pesticides and alternative agriculture/pest control practices.
- Promote learning processes where farmers and other stakeholders examine together the health, environment and other impacts of agricultural pesticides.

- Develop and make effective use of indicators for surveillance and monitoring of decreased use of chemical agricultural pesticides.
- Decrease health and environmental risks and impacts at local levels, for both farmers and consumers.
- Restore degraded local ecosystems. Ensure safe use of agricultural pesticides in diminishing quantities, according to goals established.
- Ensure high quality and safe agricultural products for local consumption.
- Improve the local economy.

3. Uganda: livestock, ecosystems and development

The issue

Livestock is a strategic export good, a key component of the modern economy and integral to indigenous range land and pastoral culture. The livestock sector contributes 5% of total GDP and 14.6% of agricultural GDP respectively (UBOS, 2004), supporting livelihoods, employment, nutrition and foreign currency earnings. Uganda's "cattle corridor," the traditional range land area, extends from the south-west through the central region to the north-east. It constitutes 44% of the country's geographical area, 40% of the national population, and 55% and 42% of the indigenous and exotic cattle species respectively. Around 60% of the households in the cattle corridor keep livestock, compared to 22% nationally. In some parts of Uganda, livestock are the primary capital reserve of households, serving as insurance against unforeseen risks and events. The Ugandan Poverty Eradication Action Plan (2005) reported that better-off households owned four times as much livestock as the poorest households, and noted this as a key factor in poverty reduction. The integration of animal husbandry and crop agriculture also has provided the main avenue for agriculture intensification in a few areas of Uganda.

The world's livestock sector is growing, with growth concentrated in developing countries, including Uganda.

Animal production growth rates (%) for major livestock products from 1990 to 1995

Commodity	Developing countries	Developed countries
Ruminant meat	4.3	-2.0
Pork	8.5	-1.2
Poultry	12.1	1.9
Milk	3.4	-1.9
Eggs	9.4	-1.5

Source: FAO-WAICENT, 1996

Markets in neighbouring, regional, Mediterranean and Middle Eastern countries are potential clients for good quality Ugandan meat provided that necessary animal health standards are met. Middle Eastern consumers, in particular, have demonstrated a willingness to pay a premium for Ugandan beef from the indigenous Ankole Longhorn and Small East African Zebu breeds, often preferred in taste and quality. However, a surplus for export requires a substantial increase in the rate of domestic production. The current 2.3% annual growth rate of Ugandan livestock numbers lags behind population growth (3.3%). Per capita availability of livestock products for the domestic market was 40 litres of milk and 5.6 kg of meat in 2001, compared to 200 litres of milk and 50 kg of meat recommended by the Food and Agriculture Organization of the United Nations (FAO) and WHO.

Low livestock sector productivity, per head of cattle, is related to: the genetic potential of local breeds; inadequate nutrition; inadequate access to water; poor access to credit; poor infrastructure and lack of market information. Sanitary requirements often block meat exports. There is no doubt that Uganda needs to adopt a market-based approach to developing the livestock sector, to stimulate competitiveness in the external market and to seize emerging opportunities in the domestic market.

Uganda's livestock development strategy, as outlined in the Plan for Modernization of Agriculture, focuses on the achievement of self-sufficiency in meat, milk and livestock products for the domestic market;

promoting export; establishing efficient livestock disease control, based on cost recovery; developing industries for dairy, leather and meat processing; and promoting research to upgrade the quality and productivity of the present breeds.

At the World Summit on Sustainable Development (WSSD) it was emphasized that improved livestock productivity and poverty reduction can best be achieved through environmentally-friendly management regimes. So far, Ugandan livestock management and planning strategies have made little explicit reference to environment and health although there are multiple links, both positive and negative. Livestock management practices affect transmission rates of animal and zoonotic diseases. Increased importation of "exotic" cattle breeds (3% of all Ugandan cattle) may improve productivity but require more intense use of agrochemicals to control disease vectors. Use of chemicals can affect the quality of livestock products, the ecosystem and human health. Unsustainable grazing practices can result in soil loss on site and siltation downstream, with long-term impacts for desertification, food security and human well-being. Further along the lifecycle chain, waste from meat processing can pollute waterbodies; and failure to meet international sanitary and food safety requirements can affect both domestic and export markets.

The goal of this project was critically to reassess Ugandan livestock management policies in light of the inextricable linkages between livestock, human health and the environment; with the aim of guiding policies that benefit health and environment while reducing poverty.

The process

The Ugandan Ministry of Water, Lands and Environment coordinated an intersectoral assessment process bringing together experts and policy-makers from several Ugandan institutions. These included the Ministry of Agriculture, Animal Industry and Fisheries; Ministry of Health; National Drug Authority, National Environment Management Authority (NEMA), Government Chemist and Analytical Laboratory and Makerere University, among others.

The results of the study were presented to the Ugandan government in a national workshop in July 2006, and at a regional workshop hosted by the Ugandan Ministers of Environment, and Minister of State for Health Care in May, 2005. The latter meeting was attended by over 40 participants from six countries from the East African region, many of which face similarly issues related to environment, health and livestock production. Participants welcomed HELI's focus on integrating health and environment considerations into economic development policy at the national level, and highlighted the benefits of linking with initiatives such as the IDRC Ecohealth programme, which has a greater focus at the community level. The meeting further recommended expanding and institutionalizing the approach, for example through a regional or continental Health and Environment forum.

Nationally, in Uganda, the HELI process has underscored the importance of multidisciplinary teamwork, integrated assessment and planning. Members of the HELI team currently are participating in the formulation of a national meat export strategy and providing multisectoral inputs to other plans, policies, laws and strategies related to the livestock sector – including the zoning of agricultural farmlands, and value chain analysis of the livestock industry.

The assessment

The assessment examined health and environment impacts along three critical points of the livestock production chain including:

- testing and evaluating chemical inputs;
- extended cost-benefit analysis (CBA) comparison of livestock management regimes;
- analysing health and environment impacts of processing livestock products, particularly abattoir- generated pollution in Lake Victoria.

The three key points of critical focus are summarized below, with conclusions and recommendations.

Assessment of chemical inputs component – filling knowledge gaps

Chemicals applied to livestock most frequently include those used to control disease vectors, such as ticks and tsetse flies. Ticks are carriers of the veterinary diseases anaplasmosis and East Coast Fever; tsetse flies are carriers of trypanosomiasis, which affects cattle and humans. Chemical use may therefore have positive impacts on health, e.g. improving animal productivity, curbing disease transmission to humans. At the same time, chemicals applied to livestock or infiltrating livestock products from the broader environment also can impact negatively on health, e.g. through residues or tainting of food products, pollution of drinking-water sources, bio-accumulation in food sources, and disease vectors' increased resistance to chemical control.

Uganda is already a signatory to the major international conventions, treaties and regulations relating to food quality, safety and the use of chemicals. Some of these have been mainstreamed nationally and the Ministry of Health is developing a Food Safety Bill and Strategic Plan as part of this process. One objective of the bill is to ensure that food safety policies and practices are harmonized with those of international trading partners, in compliance with Codex, the World Organisation for Animal Health (OIE), Integrated Pollution Control and Prevention (IPPC), World Trade Organization (WTO) and the Biosafety Protocol.

There are increasing pressures for greater chemical use in Uganda. Commercial agricultural and livestock ventures are growing and the continuing prevalence of vector-borne diseases in human populations has generated a debate about the re-introduction of DDT. These pressures, underlying health and environment issues and the need to adhere to international policy frameworks, all underline the importance of sustainable chemical use.

This exercise generated a baseline of chemical residue data associated with livestock management – where no such data existed before. These data will be used for monitoring and evaluating future development strategies, and to inform and influence decision-making. Over 170 tests for pesticide, acaricide and antibiotic residues in meat and milk products and water sources were carried out during the HELI assessment. Results of tests yielded residue levels that were low overall and below international food safety standards and drinking-water guidelines (see detailed analysis in full report).

Nonetheless, risks from food- and water-borne chemical contamination remain a concern. Between 1996 and 2001, Uganda incurred substantial economic losses through reduced earnings from fish exports as a result of fish poisoning from pesticides, as well as other food-safety problems such as outbreaks of cholera and salmonella. Presently, there are fears that the country could incur additional losses if it opts to control malaria using DDT, which bioaccumulates in animal tissues with long-term ecosystem effects and potentially important human health impacts (Rogan and Chen 2005). This debate underscores the importance of scientific knowledge and public participation in considering policy tradeoffs, in the kind of multidisciplinary framework supported by HELI.

By supporting the chemical analysis tests, the HELI project made two contributions to Uganda's health and environment knowledge base: (i) benchmarking current levels against which future policy tradeoffs may be considered; and (ii) human and institutional capacity building within the National Analytical Laboratory.

Extended CBA assessment of livestock management regimes

In addition to providing direct economic benefits, livestock generate a series of positive and negative effects on health and the environment – some of which can be valued in economic terms. In indigenous grazing systems, livestock can improve soil cover by dispersing seed through manure and with their hoofs. They control shrub growth, break up soil crusts and remove biomass – reducing the risk of bush fires, stimulating grass-tillering and improving seed germination, vegetation, soil fertility and water absorption capacity for recharging groundwater reserves. Yet recent increases in herd and human populations have increased consumption of vegetation and water resources, generating new pressures on ecosystems with associated economic costs. In Uganda, land degradation and soil loss resulting from poor livestock management (particularly poor grazing practices among pastoralists) have become an issue.

A cost-benefit analysis (CBA) tool was used to appraise four livestock management regimes, with reference to health and environment impacts. The regimes considered included:

1. purely pastoral system
2. agropastoral system (pastoral migration of cattle/some traditional agriculture)
3. semi-mixed system (settled livestock production with crop production)
4. commercially-oriented system.

The CBA was 'extended' to incorporate impacts to

HEALTH ENVIRONMENT

Direct and extended cost-benefit analysis of alternative livestock regimes

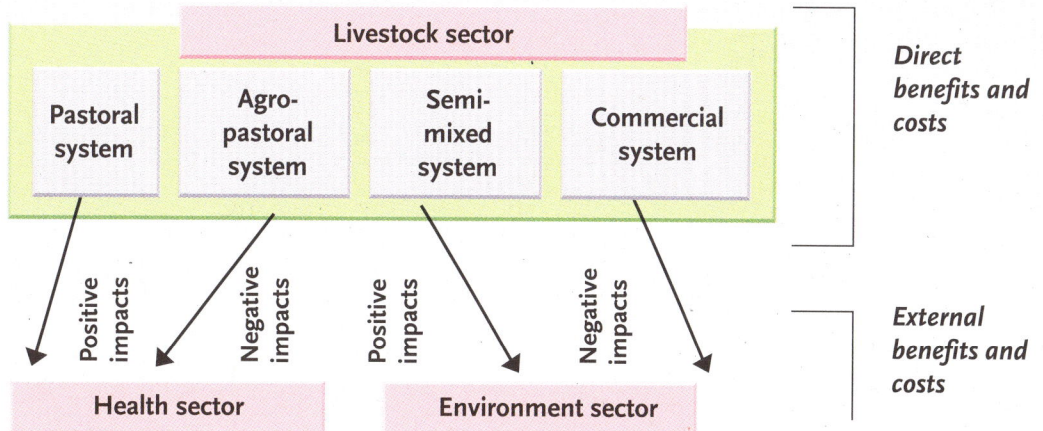

other sectors, particularly health and environment. For instance – the government, acting on behalf of society, should charge enterprises that impose costs on other sectors for related environmental clean-up and healthcare costs. Conversely, an enterprise that impacts positively on health and environment should negotiate an incentive from government e.g. tax rebates. Direct and indirect or external costs are reflected broadly in the conceptual framework above.

Following this conceptual frame, the positive and negative impacts on health and environment associated with different management regimes were catalogued.

Catalogue of main health and environment impacts of livestock on other sectors

Type of impact	Productivity impacts for other sectors (market data)		Welfare impacts on society (non-market data)	
	Health	Environment	Health	Environment
Positive impacts (benefits)		• Productivity gains provided by livestock that are enjoyed by other sectors e.g landscape benefits that impact positively on tourism industry.	• Nutritional values from consumption of livestock products.	
Negative impacts (costs)	• Productivity loss e.g. loss due to illness from livestock-borne diseases such as sleeping sickness. • Costs incurred by hospitals treating livestock-related diseases.	• Productivity losses e.g. costs to National Water and Sewerage Corporation of removing nitrate and pesticide pollution from drinking-water or for treating wastewater before discharge. • Costs to local governments of dredging stream channels and maintaining feeder roads from soil washed from overgrazed farmlands.	• Burden of livestock-borne diseases.	• Loss of ecological values (such as river quality) from pollution. • Loss of biodiversity due to pollution. • Cost of dealing with conflicts over water for domestic and livestock use. • Travel costs to find water when existing sources are polluted. • Land degradation (deforestation/ desertification) contributing to local/global climate change.

A TOOLKIT FOR DECISION-MAKERS | 74

Incorporation of health and environment externalities

Direct and indirect (external) costs and benefits can be combined into the formulation of a CBA equation:

$$NPV = B_d + B_e - C_d - C_e$$

where NPV = net present value, B_d = direct project benefits, B_e = external (health and/or environmental) benefits; C_d = direct project costs; C_e = external (health and/or environmental) costs.

Ideally, all health and environment externalities would be valued and incorporated into the analysis, quantification and valuation of this full range of costs and benefits at the scale of industrial and household livestock production enterprises. As in most cases, incomplete data precluded this option, and the team therefore opted for the following two-stage process.

- Economic valuation of the full range of direct costs of material and labour inputs and benefits (in terms of market value of agricultural products) from each management regime, expressed in terms of NPV (estimate of direct annual monetary benefits minus direct costs) and benefit-to-cost ratios. This quantitative evaluation was provided alongside qualitative description of the indirect health and environment impacts associated with each type of management system.

- Economic valuation of the total estimated cost of one of the most critical environmental externalities – costs of soil degradation – in a second stage of the process.

All four livestock management regimes generate positive NPVs and benefit:cost ratios when only direct cost are evaluated, with the commercially oriented system being the most profitable. Health and environment trade-offs are apparent in the qualitative description of impacts. For example, the pastoral system is associated with greater soil erosion and higher costs off-site for local governments – dredging stream channels and maintaining feeder roads. On the other hand, preference for exotic livestock in the commercial system may undermine the conservation of indigenous breeds, which are more resistant to local diseases and represent a value to biodiversity conservation.

Economic valuation of soil degradation

After mapping the range of externalities, the team estimated the value of one of the most important perceived external costs – soil loss and land degradation associated with poor livestock management practices in general, pastoral and agro-pastoral systems particularly.

According to the State of the Environment Report for Uganda (2000/01), overgrazing is the most important factor in soil loss and land degradation in the cattle corridor. In turn, this increases long-term risks of desertification with consequences for productivity and health. To quantify soil loss and land degradation, the team considered income foregone as a result of prior land desertification. To assign monetary value, they used a "transfer" method of economic valuation, whereby estimates of economic losses or benefits identified in one locale are applied to another similar study location.

The basis for calculating the extent of land degradation and desertification in Uganda was the drylands map prepared by the United Nations Educational, Scientific and Cultural Organization (UNESCO) in the context of Agenda 21, and still used for national estimations of drylands (UNESCO, 1997). Estimations of land use available for each respective livestock management regime in Uganda was based upon FAO Production Yearbook statistics for range lands, irrigated and rainfed croplands (FAO, 1986).

Watering cattle in a dam in Uganda: the sharing of water sources between animals and humans can have health and environment impacts.

Mapping livestock impacts on health and environment

Management regimes	Health	Environment
Scenario I: *Pastoral systems*	(+) Nutritive value of livestock products (incl. relatively lower cholesterol of meat from indigenous cattle). (-) Hospital costs/human productivity losses from livestock-related diseases like sleeping sickness. (-) Human disease through consumption of meat products lacking adequate veterinary control. (-) Long-term exposure of farmers and pastoralists to acaricides may lead to chronic health impacts.	(+) Landscape benefits for tourism. (-) Soil erosion/compaction; water contamination due to poor grazing practice. (-) High local government costs for dredging streams/ repairing roads damaged by soil erosion. (-) Silting of valley dams and tanks. (-) Loss of biodiversity from clearing, overgrazing. (-) High off-site costs to government for controlling and treating water and waste discharge. (-) Widespread animal-borne diseases.
Scenario II: *Agropastoral systems*	(+) Nutritive value of livestock products (incl. relatively lower cholesterol of meat from indigenous cattle). (-) Human disease through meat consumption. (-) Hospital costs/human productivity losses livestock-related diseases like sleeping sickness. (-) Long-term exposure of farmers and pastoralists to acaricides may lead to health impacts.	(+) Landscape benefits for tourism. (-) Soil compaction/erosion, water contamination due to poor grazing practice.
Scenario III: *Mixed systems*	(+) Nutritive value of livestock products (including relatively higher milk production of exotic cattle breeds). (-) Chemicals can cause acute poisoning and be used for suicides. (-) Long-term exposure of farmers and pastoralists to acaricides may lead to health impacts. (-) Human disease through meat consumption. (-) Hospital costs/human productivity losses from livestock-related diseases like sleeping sickness.	(+) Waste products (manure) can be controlled and used more efficiently to enrich soils for agriculture. (+) Nutrient recycling – e.g. in soils and in fodder for animals. (-) Soil erosion and water/air pollution. Soil compaction. (-) Substitution of exotic breeds for indigenous leads to loss of genetic resources, (e.g. resistance to disease of indigenous breeds).
Scenario IV: *Commercial systems* (including zero grazing fenced farms)	(+) Nutritive value of livestock products (including relatively higher milk production of exotic cattle breeds). (-) High local water consumption reduces water available for human consumption/hygiene. (-) Chemicals can cause acute poisoning and be used for suicides. (-) Long-term exposure of acaricides creates chronic health effects. (-) Overuse of accumulated manure can intensify heavy metal accumulation of soil and crops. (-) Human disease through meat consumption. (-) Hospital costs/human productivity losses for livestock-related diseases like sleeping sickness.	(+) Waste products (manure) can be controlled and used more efficiently to enrich soils. (+) Nutrient recycling may be more efficient, e.g. through animal fodder and into soils. (-) Concentrated feed production affects land and water quality. (-) Greater use of fossil fuels in livestock production. (-) Substitution of exotic breeds for indigenous leads to loss of genetic resources, (e.g. resistance to disease of indigenous breeds). (-) Deforestation, soil erosion, soil compaction and air/water pollution can result from expansion of commercial farms over large areas.

Note: *This is a preliminary and indicative listing of potential impacts. Further evaluation would be required to more precisely rank or order impacts, in each management regime, and with respect to the other regimes. In addition, while some health and environment impacts, e.g. nutrition benefits, are cross-cutting to all regimes, others, e.g. heavy metal accumulation in manure, are more closely identified with one regime.*

Costs of desertification in Uganda

Type	Desertification estimates in dry lands (000 ha)						% desertification	Annual costs (US$ 000)	Total costs (US$ 000)
		Slight	Moderate	Severe	Very severe	Total moderate+			
Irrigated	16	15	1	0	0	1	6	250	250
Rainfed	834	294	440	80	20	540	65	38	20 520
Range land	8561	461	500	7500	100	8100	95	7	56 700
Total	9411	770	941	7580	120	8641			**77 470**

Local Ugandan data on unit costs of land degradation were aggregated on the basis of a model of American and Australian studies on the unit costs of land degradation and desertification in irrigated, rainfed and range land agriculture. Based on these inputs and measured by income foregone, the estimates of annual costs of desertification in Uganda were estimated to total US$ 77.47 million, including US$ 56.70 for range lands, US$ 20.51 million for rainfed cropland, and only US$ 0.250 million for irrigated croplands, as detailed above.

While there were insufficient data for precise quantification, it was the conservative estimate of the team that at least 30% of this land degradation cost may be attributed to poor grazing and livestock management practices, based upon quantitative and qualitative evidence of current grazing and livestock practices. It was thus estimated that poor livestock management practices generate a total cost of at least US$ 22 million annually in terms of foregone benefits, due to land degradation and desertification.

This estimate of US$ 22 million in annual losses greatly exceeds net foreign exchange earnings from exports of livestock products. In 2003 these foreign exchange earnings were estimated to be at least US$ 4.9 million per annum.

This is a serious concern given that soil fertility and land resources are mainstays of the agricultural economy and livelihoods for the poor, and degradation increases the risk of desertification. Moreover, unless pastoralists are educated to improve their grazing practices, such losses will continue. Reflecting these concerns, the Poverty Eradication Action Plan (PEAP) 2004/5-2007/8 has noted: "there has been only limited uptake of 'improved' livestock technologies to meet the needs of livestock keepers in general and pastoralists in particular."

Assessment of pollution risks from slaughterhouses

The risk to health and environment that may be associated with pollution discharges from slaughterhouses and meat processing plants into Lake Victoria was the final issue considered in this analysis. Pollution discharges are a direct health and environment concern as drinking-water supplies for the capital city of Kampala are drawn from the lake by the National Water and Sewerage Corporation. Since 1996 the joint World Bank/Global Environment Facility (GEF) funded Lake Victoria Environmental Management Project has been monitoring pollution emissions from hot spots in urban areas. Resulting estimates of net annual discharges, after emissions have passed through wetlands, river systems and other natural purification systems, are summarized below.

Pollution loading reaching Lake Victoria (Kg/day)

Point source type	BOD Biological oxygen demand	TN Total nitrates	TP Total phosphates
Urban centres	14 166 (76%)	2911 (83%)	1932 (89%)
Fishing villages	2 000 (11%)	251 (7%)	131 (6%)
Industry	2 513 (13%)	339 (10%)	105 (5%)
Totals	18 679	3501	2168

Of the industrial contribution, an estimated 10% to 40% of the pollution load is from abattoirs and meat-packing industry near the lake, depending on the type of pollution considered.

Pollution loading from abattoirs and meat-packers (Kg/day)

	BOD Biological oxygen demand	COD Chemical oxygen demand	TSS Total suspended solids	TN Total nitrates	TP Total phosphates	NH_3 Ammonia	Receiving unit
Total industrial pollution load	6980	16 005	6542	2119	410	198	Nakivubo wetland
Contribution of abattoirs and meat-packers	10%	13%	40%	8%	16%	31%	Nakivubo wetland

Since discharges do not pass through the central sewage treatment system, the team could not estimate the costs associated with treatment before discharge. However, costs of treatment following discharge are absorbed indirectly by the Government which has leveraged loans and invested up to US$ 1.49 million on wetlands conservation around Lake Victoria. Despite this, considerable deterioration of water quality has been observed which inevitably will require further ecosystem restoration or water-treatment expense.

Connection between livestock, water quality and health

Pollution emissions alter the ecosystem balance in Lake Victoria. This has been associated with the increasing frequency and intensity of thick blooms of toxic blue-green algae, particularly around Murchison Bay where drinking-water for Kampala and the surrounding urban areas is drawn. Such algal blooms are toxic to humans and animals. In particular, cyanobacteria accumulate in fish tissues and have been found to poison wild animals such as fish, kangaroos and birds (Krienitz et. al., 2003). Human impacts may include skin and eye irritations, diarrhoea, disorders of the nervous system, and liver damage.

A study of cyanobacteria was conducted by the Canadian International Development Agency (CIDA), in collaboration with the Fisheries Resources Research Institute (FIRRI) and the National Water and Sewage Corporation (NWSC). This found highly toxic blue-green scum (Microcystis and Anabaena spp.) and water hyacinth clustered along the shore near two major Kampala city drinking-water intake sites. The study concludes that NWSC water-treatment facilities are generally adequate for removing algae from their intake water. However, while conventional water-treatment works can remove algae, usually they cannot remove the toxins released from burst or dying cells in some blue-green algae. In such a scenario, toxins released could surpass water-treatment capacities, potentially exposing the residents of Kampala to moderate levels of microcystins.

In addition, many people in the rural areas use water directly from the Lake Victoria shoreline for domestic purposes. Toxic cyanobacteria are present there at dangerous levels and must be assumed to be having negative health effects on the lakeshore communities and livestock of Lake Victoria (CIDA 2002).

Algal blooms not only increase health risks, but also raise the expense of water treatment by clogging filters on pumps and machinery, increasing chlorine demand, leading to increased trihalomethane (THM) precursors which lead to increased chloroform and other potential carcinogens in treated water supplies. The potential health risk and the concomitant high costs of treatment highlight the need for better pre-discharge control measures by all polluters.

Some industries along Lake Victoria already have embraced strategies for better wastewater management and treatment, known as cleaner production mechanisms (CPM). This approach could be extended to livestock-related industries which contribute a substantial load of industrial waste to the lake.

Often pollution-control measures represent a purely positive outcome for environment, business and health, as evidenced in a sample of experiences cited below.

Cleaner production benefits in Uganda

Company	Benefits
Mukwano Industries Ltd.	• Water consumption reduced by 10% • Materials economized (US$ 564) • Electricity consumption reduced by 20%
Ngege Ltd.	• Water consumption reduced by 30.5% • Overall yield increase from 38% to 41% • BOD reduction from 341 mg/l to 90mg/l • COD reduction from 874mg/l to 140mg/l
Kakira Sugar Works Ltd.(sugar factory)	• Water consumption reduced by 43% • BOD reduction from 1000 mg to 600mg/l • Improved work conditions (temperature, noise, light)

Source: Uganda Cleaner Production Centre, 2002

Conclusions and recommendations

The study generated a series of important new insights into environment, health and development planning in the livestock industry in Uganda. One of the key goals of the National Environment Management Policy for Uganda is to: "... integrate environmental costs and benefits into economic planning and development at all levels of government in order to reflect the true costs and benefits of development." The HELI project provided the first opportunity to test out such an approach in Uganda. It demonstrated that the economic performances of certain sectors may be overstated if they are not adjusted to consider their negative impacts on other sectors, most importantly health and environment.

An overall conclusion of this study is the need for government to reappraise the competitiveness of the livestock sub-sector from a market-based approach, involving a full understanding of the external and internal factors influencing growth and competitiveness.

By looking at various critical points in the livestock production chain, important impacts to environment and to health were identified and, in some cases (e.g. land degradation), valued economically. The initiative supported a small-scale survey of agrochemical residues in meat, milk and water bodies in Uganda. The findings offer some reassurance that chemical contamination of food may not be a major hazard in the Ugandan livestock industry. However, larger surveys that focus on likely hot spots are necessary to give full confidence. The equipment and capacity building supported by HELI will help this process.

The study showed that different livestock management systems have very different implications for health and the environment. Although commercial livestock systems have the highest benefit/cost ratio for direct economic costs, a series of important health and environment externalities, such as soil compaction and erosion, could make alternatives such as mixed farm systems more cost-beneficial overall. These effects can be very large: the estimated annual costs of land degradation from poor livestock management are estimated at US$ 22 million annually, a cost far exceeding the value of livestock exports.

Fishermen on Lake Victoria's shores. The flow of untreated sewage into the lake from slaughterhouses and other industries can impact health and environment directly and indirectly - lowering drinking water quality and stimulating toxic algae blooms that accumulate in fish tissues.

All stages of the livestock production cycle generate health and environment effects: abattoirs and meat-packers discharge a large proportion of pollution into Lake Victoria around Kampala. This incurs indirect costs to the government and generates new health risks, for example via toxins from blue-green algae.

The national team made the following key recomendations for national policy development in the livestock sector:

A multisectoral approach to food and chemical safety

- Members of the HELI study team should support further development of a multisectoral approach to the revision and updating of all related food and chemical safety laws, policies, strategies and guidelines. This should include efforts to raise awareness, sensitizing and educating local communities and policy-makers about the positive and negative health and environment impacts of chemical use.

- Ongoing monitoring of chemical residues should be included in the government's bi-ennial 'State of the Environment Report'.

- Uganda should study the growing global demand for organic food products and formulate policies to tap a small, but growing and potentially high-value, market sector.

Improved agroecological zoning and pastoral land management

- Zoning of agricultural production should be in line with agroecological conditions, so as to reduce land degradation and risks of desertification, within the framework of existing proposals contained in the Strategic Exports Programme.

- As provided in the National Environment Act Guidelines, NEMA should issue guidelines for the sustainable management of range lands (where most livestock activities take place). These should be part of a broader effort to educate pastoralists about sustainable range-land management.

- Water resources should be zoned for livestock or human consumption in order to minimize the risks of zoonotic disease transmission.

- Sustained intensification of mixed farming systems should be promoted. Even though commercial farming shows a higher benefit to cost ratio when only the direct costs of labour and materials and benefits of sales of products are quantified, mixed farming may be more cost-beneficial when all health and environmental externalities are valued fully. Mixed farming systems should thus be encouraged to optimize livestock's economic benefits for livelihoods, health and the environment but limit negative impacts.

Assessment of industry operations and support for CPM

- Conduct a full cost-benefit analysis of risks to health and aquatic biodiversity resulting from livestock pollution emissions into Lake Victoria.

- The results of this analysis should be used to support better waste and wastewater treatment, disposal and management in the framework of CPM and economic measures, ensuring that health and environment costs are borne by polluters rather than the government or the general public.

More generally, there is a need for further capacity building in the use of analytical decision tools like CBA, cost-effectiveness analysis and multi-criteria analysis to support decision-making in strategic sectors of the economy including the livestock sector. Finally, the project has highlighted a need for more education about aspects of intersectoral linkages and their economic impacts at policy and technical levels.

For more information and full report see:

Uganda: livestock, ecosystems and development. Ministry of Water, Lands and Environment, Kampala, 2006.

www.who.int/heli/pilots/uganda/en/

VII. CONCLUSION
Consolidating health and environment linkages: a contribution to global policy agendas

New understandings about the mounting risks to health of ecosystem degradation, and positive contributions to health from ecosystem services, mandate a fresh approach to health and environment in this new millennium. This should contribute to the achievements of the Millennium Development Goals and the WSSD Plan of Implementation, and respond to global leaders at the 2005 World Summit on UN reform who requested greater system-wide coherence throughout the United Nations.

Since its launch at WSSD, HELI has been a practical example of how such aims can be put into practice, forging an active global-level partnership between WHO and UNEP and creating a platform for joint health and environment policy assessment and action at country level.

HELI is not the only example of such coordination, nor is it the first such initiative. In Europe, for instance, a regional process of dialogue and actions involving ministries of health and environment has been active since the late 1980s. In the Americas, more recent collaboration between ministers of health and environment also has yielded many fruitful synergies.

But it does bring important new dimensions. HELI's efforts have focused on new applications of linked approaches in Asia, Africa and the eastern Mediterranean regions, and on global dissemination of guidance, methodological tools and good practice experiences. By harnessing the wealth of existing knowledge on environment and health, HELI has sought to make the business case for linkage between the sectors at country level. Rather than generating new research, the initiative has demonstrated a management method for national ministries to make better use of available evidence – through linked assessment of health and environmental impacts and costs and benefits – which supports evidence-based policies and economic development strategies.

1. Reconciling fragmented approaches

HELI's experience has the potential for wider replication within the broader context of UN reform. Health and environment issues cross sectors at global level as they do at local and country level. United Nations activities, from normative to operational, increasingly have emphasized the need to address adequately the links between health and environment.

Growing recognition of the relevance of such linkages provides the UN system with a unique opportunity to stimulate and support synergistic strategies for sustainable development. Such strategies ensure greater effectiveness of programmes, maximize the use of limited resources and increase impacts on decision-making.

Building upon the successful partnership and collaboration that has developed over the past decade, UNEP and WHO should continue to develop a strategic approach for joint actions on environment and health within the broader development context. Designed and implemented in close cooperation with a range of actors at global, regional and national levels, the strategy should aim to improve coordination and cooperation among existing initiatives and approaches, identify gaps, reduce duplications and maximize institutional efficiency. As a contribution to such an effort, some proposed strategic goals and objectives drawn from the HELI experience are noted in the table below.

Towards a consolidated health and environment agenda: strategic objectives

1) Facilitate synthesis of evidence-based methodologies and tools for informed policy decisions.

    (a) *Promote health and environment impacts as integral to economic development processes* at all stages of global, regional and, particularly, country level policy formulation. Encourage integration of health and environment objectives with poverty reduction strategies (PRSPs) and regional development plans, including investments related to sectoral economic activities.

    (b) *Support policy assessment of the linked health and environment costs and benefits, integrating qualitative methods* (e.g. stakeholder dialogue deliberative assessment) with quantitative tools (e.g. burden of disease assessment and economic valuation).

(c) *Facilitate global, regional and national monitoring/surveillance of linked health and environment trends and policy responses as well as **integrated collections and analysis of data and indicators on health and environment**.*

(d) ***Coordinate scientific and technical reviews*** *by health and environment experts to define priorities and identify knowledge gaps as well as **refine normative health and environment standards and guidelines**.*

(e) ***Refine and improve systems for effective health and environment preparedness*** *and response to emergencies, conflicts and disasters, including assessment, prevention crisis intervention, and planning for post-emergency reconstruction.*

(f) ***Support applied research, particularly at the local level,*** *to build technical capacity, strengthen cooperation among key actors and answer practical policy questions.*

2) **Promote knowledge sharing, outreach and advocacy for enhanced capacity**

(a) ***Synthesize and disseminate research, case studies and good practice experiences*** *that highlight win-win development strategies and make scientific knowledge easily accessible to policy-makers and stakeholders.*

(b) ***Support professional capacity-building and intersectoral workshops*** *to encourage decision-makers, professionals from various sectors and stakeholders to share knowledge, exchange views and reflect on new information which otherwise they would not have time to review.*

(c) ***Support good practices at individual, household and community levels*** *that improve the immediate environment using low-cost, available and tested interventions, e.g. for safe household water collection or storage; improved sanitation, integrated vector management and indoor air pollution.*

(d) ***Expand "healthy settings" approaches*** *that holistically address a range of risks in the urban, employment, market or school environment across sectors.*

(e) ***Scale up communications and advocacy globally, fostering broad public and targeted groups' awareness*** *of the state of the linkages and emerging threats; impact on vulnerable populations (particularly children); and successful practices and models of interventions and experiences highlighting the multiple benefits of integrated interventions and participatory approaches.*

3) **Facilitate and promote alliances and partnerships for coherent and coordinated actions.**

(a) ***Develop a health and environment forum.*** *This should be multi-stakeholder and multidisciplinary, designed as a central platform where partnerships and initiatives involving health, environment and development sectors converge. It would review topical health and environment issues; facilitate science to policy dialogue; increase use of decision-making tools and methodologies; and strengthen global coordination and effective response to promote health through better environmental management.*

(b) ***Enhance coordination and collaboration with the existing UN system interagency policy and programme coordinating mechanisms,*** *such as the United Nations Environment Management Group (UNEMG) to facilitate the design of complementary environmental, social and economic policies in response to implementation plans for sustainable development.*

(c) ***Strengthen joint WHO/UNEP cooperation*** *on health and environment issues in the framework of existing and new partnerships with:*

- *intergovernmental development and cooperation agencies – forging common programmes, projects and policy agendas;*
- *research and academic institutions – identifying emerging risks and improved practices and approaches;*
- *private sector – identifying synergies between scientific knowledge, technological innovation and sustainable patterns of production and consumption;*
- *civil society – promoting and sharing knowledge from global to individual level.*

2. Repositioning health and environment sectors towards proactive policies

For too long, both health and environment sectors have sought to cope with the downstream consequences of poorly-conceived policies –pollution, environmental degradation and ill-health – while having little influence on upstream decisions that profoundly shape the human and natural environment.

Increasingly, health actors are recognizing how multiple economic, social and institutional drivers impact on environment risks and, as a result, health status and the demand for health services. These drivers range from the pressures of a globalized economy to the insecurities of poverty, political instability and labour markets, along with new opportunities arising from fast-evolving technologies, increased human mobility and new scientific knowledge.

In this dynamic landscape, a health sector that focuses solely on disease treatment and health care delivery is no longer an option. Prevention has always been the best medicine, and prevention of environmental health risks must be accorded increased emphasis in light of new knowledge about the environmental burden of disease. Environmental health must be repositioned as the preventive arm of public health. Primary environmental health interventions that reduce exposures to key pollutants or mitigate risks should be integrated into strategies for health promotion, public health practice and primary health care. But environmental health policy-making should extend beyond the health sector to address the upstream issues of ecosystem health and pollution control and abatement, reaffirming that health is: "a state of complete physical, mental and social well-being" that relies on the sustainability of life-supporting ecosystems.

Similarly, the work of the environment sector in protecting and ensuring the sustainability of ecosystems, along with the goods and services they provide, no longer can be perceived as an issue of nature conservation in the narrow sense. It is an issue of human well-being – recognizing that human health is intertwined inextricably with that of the broader natural environment. Sustainable development can best be actualized in economic plans and policies if the environment and health impacts of alternative development scenarios are recognized explicitly.

Decision-makers are far more likely to opt for environmentally sustainable modes of development when the health and environment costs of alternative policies are valued fully in terms of natural resource depletion/conservation, human mortality and morbidity, costs in health care, lost wages, etc. Health and environment sectors both recognize that economic arguments increasingly are critical to making the case for sound investment and development policies.

3: Critical link to the achievement of global development priorities

The success of current UN reform will be measured by its capacity not only to streamline bureaucracies and budgets, but also to implement policies that break the vicious cycle linking poverty, environmental degradation, ill-health and the continued inequities related to gender and vulnerable groups.

Scientists examine drinking water quality in a Burkino Faso laboratory.

HEALTH ENVIRONMENT

Solar panels provide a healthy source of renewable energy at this Médecins Sans Frontières and reduce space before "health compound in the Sudan.

Action at junctures of health and environment linkage is critical to meeting this challenge. For instance, approximately 4 million out of the nearly 12 million child deaths annually are due to diseases associated with just four main environmental health risks – indoor air pollution, unsafe water and inadequate sanitation, unintentional injuries (including traffic injuries) and malaria (Prüss-Üstün and Corvalán 2006). In turn, these risks are very largely a result of unsustainable development policies related to water resources, agriculture, land use (urban and rural), transport and energy. These driving forces must be addressed, and development policies integrating health and environment impacts implemented, in order to reduce child mortality significantly.

It is the disadvantaged and vulnerable socioeconomic groups, such as children, the poor, indigenous populations and informal workers who bear the brunt of the health impacts from environmental pollution and ecosystem degradation. Addressing health, environment and economic development issues in an interrelated manner will generate new synergies in poverty reduction and social equity. Such interventions not only minimize pollution exposures, but also harness and optimize essential ecosystem goods and services (e.g. biological control of pests and vectors; biological mechanisms for water purification) upon which the poor, in particular, depend for health and well-being. Ultimately, all social sectors gain from a broader, long-term approach that contains health costs and preserves natural resources.

Building capacity at country level remains a key factor in determining the success of a long-term and integrated approach to development. Often, governments and society wake up to a hazard only when a long-standing environmental risk erupts into a health, economic or political emergency. By moving from a reactive to a proactive policy approach, risks that might develop into full-scale environment and health emergencies can be mitigated, limiting or even preventing crises that otherwise might cripple a country's economic, political and physical infrastructure.

The UN reform process emerged in part from a growing concern that, all too often, global agendas and country actions falter as a result of institutional rivalries, potentially leading to a waste of resources and duplication of efforts. The strong and direct UNEP-WHO collaboration under HELI has proven to be highly effective in overcoming the challenges of fragmented knowledge in environment and health risks and catalysing concrete actions at the country level, by providing a science-based management model that has great potential for replication.

HELI has filled vital niches in WHO's preventive and public health agenda and in UNEP's capacity-building priorities and environment-for-development agenda by bringing health, environment and non-health sector decision-makers to the same table. It is now time to reach out to a wider audience and expand the partnership, to demonstrate further the relevance of joint and practical actions on health and environment in responding to the implementation imperatives posed by the World Summit on Sustainable Development and the United Nations Millenium Development Goals.

REFERENCES

1. CIDA (2002). *Cyanobacteria monitoring on Lake Victoria.* Ottawa, Canadian International Development Agency Youth Internship Programme.
2. Corvalán C, Briggs D & Zielhuis G, eds (2000). *Decision-making in environmental health: from evidence to action.* Geneva, World Health Organization.
3. Davenport C, Mathers J & Parry J (2006). Use of health impact assessment in incorporating health considerations in decision making. *Journal of Epidemiology and Community Health*, 60(3):196-201.
4. DFID/EC/UNDP/WorldBank (2002). *Linking poverty reduction and environmental management: policy challenges and opportunities.* Washington D.C., World Bank.
5. Esrey S (1996). Water, waste and well-being: a multi-country study. *American Journal of Epidemiology*, 143(6):608-623.
6. Esrey S et al. (1991). Effects of improved water supply and sanitation on ascariasis, diarrhoea, dracunculiasis, hookworm infection, schistosomiasis, and trachoma. *Bulletin of the World Health Organization*, 69(5):609-621.
7. Esrey SA, Feachem RG & Hughes JM (1985). Interventions for the control of diarrhoeal diseases among young children: improving water supplies and excreta disposal facilities. *Bull World Health Organ*, 63(4):757-72.
8. FAO (1986). FAO production yearbook. Rome, Food and Agriculture Organization.
9. FAO-WAICENT (1996). *Agricultural production and trade data.* Rome, Food and Agriculture Organization, World Agricultural Information Centre.
10. Gallup J & Sachs J (2001). The economic burden of malaria. *American Journal of Tropical Medicine and Hygiene*, 64(1-2 Suppl.):85-96.
11. Gubler DJ (2004). The changing epidemiology of yellow fever and dengue, 1900 to 2003: full circle? *Comparative Immunology, Microbiology and Infectious Diseases*, 27(5):319-30.
12. Howard G & Bartram J (2003). *Domestic water quantity, service level and health.* Geneva, World Health Organization (WHO/SDE/WSH/03.02).
13. Hutton G & Haller L (2004). *Evaluation of the costs and benefits of water and sanitation improvements at the global level.* Geneva, World Health Organization (WHO/SDE/WSH/04.04).
14. IPM Danida (2003). *Did you take your poison today?* Bangkok, Integrated Pest Control: Danish International Development Assistance (DANIDA).
15. Jungbluth F (1996). *Crop protection policy in Thailand: Economic and political factors influencing pesticide use. Pesticide Policy Project Publication Series No. 5.* Hannover, University of Hannover.
16. Keiser J, Singer BH & Utzinger J (2005). Reducing the burden of malaria in different eco-epidemiological settings with environmental management: a systematic review. *The Lancet Infectious Diseases*, 5(11):695-708.
17. Krienitz L et al. (2003). Contribution of hot spring cyanobacteria to the mysterious deaths of lesser flamingos at Lake Bogoria, Kenya. *FEMS Microbiology Ecology*, 43:141-148.
18. Mahoney M & Durham G (2002). *Health impact assessment: a tool for policy development in Australia. Report for Commonwealth Department for Health and Ageing.* Melbourne, Australia, Faculty of Health and Behavioural Science, Deakin University.
19. Mörner J et al. (2002). *Reducing and eliminating the use of persistent organic pesticides: guidance on alternative strategies for sustainable pest and vector management.* Geneva, IOMC.
20. Muksuwan W (2005). *The situation of agricultural pesticide application in Thailand.* Bangkok, Alternative Agricultural Network.
21. Nantulya V & Reich M (2002). The neglected epidemic: road traffic injuries in developing countries. *British Medical Journal*, 324(7346):1139-41.
22. OECD (2003). *Trends in environmental expenditure and international commitments for the environment in Eastern Europe, Caucasus and Central Asia, 1996-2001.* Kiev, United Nations Economic Commission for Europe.

23. Patz JA et al. (2005). Impact of regional climate change on human health. *Nature*, 438(7066):310-7.
24. Peden M et al., eds (2004). *World report on road traffic injury prevention*. Geneva, World Health Organization.
25. Poapongsakorn N, Ruhs M & Tangjitwisuth S (1998). Problems and outlook of agriculture in Thailand. *TDRI Quarterly Review*, 13(2):3-14.
26. Prüss-Üstün A et al. (2003-2005). *Environmental burden of disease series*. Geneva, World Health Organization.
27. Prüss-Üstün A & Corvalán C (2006). *Preventing disease through healthy environments - towards an estimate of the environmental burden of disease*. Geneva, World Health Organization.
28. Research Center of Applied Economics (2001). *Project of economic assessment and sustainable knowledge transfer in the Agricultural School Programme*. Kasetsart, Faculty of Economics, Kasetsart University.
29. Research Institute for Health Sciences (2004). *The situation of agricultural pesticides applications in north region, Thailand*. Bangkok, Research and Development Programme on Healthy Public Policy and Health Impact Assessment, Health System Research Institute (HSRI).
30. Rodsawad J et al. (2006). *Environment and health impact assessment of agricultural pesticide application for policy decision support*. Bangkok, Thai Ministry of Public Health and Health Systems Research Institute.
31. Rogan WJ & Chen AM (2005). Health risks and benefits of bis(4-chlorophenyl)-1,1,1-trichloroethane (DDT). *Lancet*, 366(9487):763-773.
32. Sachs J & Malaney P (2002). *The economic and social burden of malaria*. Nature 415: 680-685.
33. Smith K, Corvalán C & Kjellstrom T (1999). How much global ill health is attributable to environmental factors? *Epidemiology*, 10(5):573-84.
34. UN (2003). *World urbanization prospects: the 2003 revision*. New York, United Nations Department of Economic and Social Affairs - Population Division.
35. UNEP (2005). Emerging challenges - new findings: emerging and re-emerging infectious diseases: links to environmental change. *GEO yearbook 2004/5: an overview of our changing environment*. Nairobi, United Nations Environment Programme:72-79.
36. UNESCO (1979). *Map of the world distribution of arid regions*. Paris, United Nations Educational, Scientific and Cultural Organization.
37. USEPA (2005). *New York City: watershed management for urban water supply. Case Studies in Integrated Water & Coastal Resource Management*. Washington, D.C.
38. Utzinger J et al. (2002). The economic payoffs of integrated malaria control in the Zambian copperbelt between 1930 and 1950. *Tropical Medicine and International Health*, 7(8):657-77.
39. Utzinger J, Tozan Y & Singer BH (2001). Efficacy and cost-effectiveness of environmental management for malaria control. *Tropical Medicine and International Health*, 6(9):677-87.
40. WHO (2002). *The World Health Report 2002 - reducing risks, promoting healthy life*. Geneva, World Health Organization.
41. WHO (2004a). *The World Health Report 2004 - changing history*. Geneva, World Health Organization.
42. WHO (2004b). *The WHO recommended classification of pesticides by hazard and guidelines to classification*. Geneva, World Health Organization.
43. WHO (2005). *Ecosystems and human well-being, health synthesis. Millennium Ecosystem Assessment*. Geneva, World Health Organization.
44. WHO (2006). *Fuel for life: household energy and health*. Geneva, World Health Organization.
45. WRI (2005). *Ecosystems and human well-being synthesis. Millennium Ecosystem Assessment*. Washington D.C., World Resources Institute/Island Press.

For further information on the HELI initiative please contact:

The WHO/UNEP
Health and Environment Linkages Initiative Secretariat
World Health Organization
20, Avenue Appia
CH-1211 Geneva 27
Email: http://www.who.int/phe

www.unep.org

United Nations Environment Programme
P.O.Box 30552 Nairobi, Kenya
Tel: (254 2) 621234
Fax: (254 2) 623927
E-mail: cpiinfo@unep.org
web: www.unep.org

ISBN 9-2415637-2-7